The
Continuous
Appetite™

UNDERSTANDING YOUR CRAVINGS, ENDING YOUR OVEREATING!

SOPHIE SKOVER- FRABOTTA

BALBOA.PRESS

A DIVISION OF HAY HOUSE

Balboa Press books may be ordered through booksellers or by contacting:

Balboa Press
A Division of Hay House
1663 Liberty Drive
Bloomington, IN 47403
www.balboapress.com
844-682-1282

Because of the dynamic nature of the Internet, any web addresses or links contained in this book may have changed since publication and may no longer be valid. The views expressed in this work are solely those of the author and do not necessarily reflect the views of the publisher, and the publisher hereby disclaims any responsibility for them.

The author of this book does not dispense medical advice or prescribe the use of any technique as a form of treatment for physical, emotional, or medical problems without the advice of a physician, either directly or indirectly. The intent of the author is only to offer information of a general nature to help you in your quest for emotional and spiritual well-being. In the event you use any of the information in this book for yourself, which is your constitutional right, the author and the publisher assume no responsibility for your actions.

Any people depicted in stock imagery provided by Getty Images are models, and such images are being used for illustrative purposes only.
Certain stock imagery © Getty Images.

Print information available on the last page.

ISBN: 978-1-4525-4462-5 (sc)
ISBN: 978-1-4525-4464-9 (hc)
ISBN: 978-1-4525-4463-2 (e)

Library of Congress Control Number: 2011963548

Balboa Press rev. date: 02/18/2021

To My Mom—Georgie

Everything I know,
I've learned from you!

I love you—Sophie

Table of Contents

—Part One—

FACING YOUR ISSUES WITH FOOD

—Part Two—

HEALING YOUR INNER ISSUES

Checklist: Do I have The Continuous Appetite?

Have you ever said to yourself…

1. *I can't eat that because, if I do, I'll eat the whole thing!*
2. *It's too hard to lose weight.*
3. *It's ok, just eat it—I give you permission to be bad.*
4. *I don't care anymore; I'm eating it.*
5. *If I could just lose this (#) pounds, my life would be better.*
6. *Well, I've blown it. I might as well eat whatever I want now.*
7. *I'll start my diet on Monday.*
8. *Have another serving; more will taste even better.*
9. *I've had a bad day, so now I'm going to eat whatever I want.*
10. *Everything is out of my control; I might as well EAT.*
11. *I can't believe I ate the whole thing.*
12. *I want to lose weight but, by the end of the day, I give up.*
13. *I'm fat; no one likes me.*
14. *I lose weight during the week and gain it all back over the weekend.*
15. *I ate too much; now I need to throw up.*
16. *Why do I have to struggle with food?*
17. *I wish I were addicted to drugs rather than food, because then I could just quit my addiction once and for all.*
18. *Sometimes I wake up in the middle of the night and eat.*
19. *My cravings are so strong that I panic and end up overeating.*
20. *When I'm by myself, I get fast food and pig out in my car.*

21. *I've tried every diet out there, but nothing works.*

22. *I want to eat all the time; not from hunger, but from cravings.*

...If you said "yes" to three or more, keep reading and you will learn how to heal the continuous appetite.

How Healing Will Happen

"My cravings are so strong. I panic, overeat, and then feel horrible about myself!" This is what my struggle with the continuous appetite sounded like for years, and I didn't even know it was happening. To some extent, we all have it: that continuous state of anxiety, dissatisfaction, and numbness that overwhelms life. Until this point, you may have thought that food was the problem but, instead, **food has actually been a survival method that is no longer working for you**. In fact, it's working against you. Now is the time to stop and acknowledge that your soul found food as a way through the darkness. Unfortunately that "way" has led you to this even darker place, but you wouldn't be here if you weren't ready to heal.

The very fact that you are reading this book shows that you're ready to stop using food to silence your inner issues, negative thoughts, painful situations, physical disharmony, spiritual imbalances, and uncomfortable feelings. You have come to a great place, one that is going to uncover all the gunk that is creating garbage in your life and, if you practice the techniques outlined in this book, all that toxic trash will finally disappear. What you will learn here is that your food cravings are just an indicator that **something within is off balance**. This process will help you find out what the core problem is, teach you what to do with it, and heal your inner issues without using food as a false solution.

THE CONTINUOUS APPETITE is based on healing your inner issues one craving at a time. Your first assignment is to face what comes up within you and do so **one** issue at a time. As Rome wasn't built in a day, your healing will not happen instantaneously. Instead, you'll learn that your cravings are signals that something is "off" deep within your body, emotions, mind and spirit, and you will be given necessary tools to practice different approaches that bring every aspect of yourself back into balance. It's no accident that you have come to this place (right where you are at this moment) in order to receive healing and, if you open up to this journey, and do so at your own pace, I promise that you'll be free from the continuous appetite.

At the end of each chapter, you will be asked to complete an assignment. These exercises are the tools that I discovered that took me from eating disordered to eating mindfully and freely. I encourage you to complete them at your own pace, and realize that some of them will be easier for you than others. Why? Because the exercises are designed to help you look at yourself little by little. What you unlock over time is what you are being asked to look at now and, the goal is for you to learn from and work on these self-revelations as they reveal themselves. I encourage you to try to not rush through this book, but rather read it at your own pace and allow new awareness to sink in.

Everything happens for a reason and, right now, in this moment, you're in the perfect place. Although you may feel a little battered and chaotic, you have come to this special place within yourself to learn some great life lessons. Healing is on its way to you and, by completing this process one craving at a time, you will someday turn back and see just how far you have traveled from this imbalanced place. If this ultimate victory sounds like something you want, I encourage you to read further. Take your time, do the work, and—most important—be open to the discoveries that come your way. If at any point you need assistance in working through some issues, reach out to a professional. If you get stuck, there are counselors, life coaches, psychologists, and therapists who know how best to help you.

I have one last question for you as your self-discovery journey begins: Are you ready to receive a quality of life that includes health on all levels including body wellbeing, emotional balance, mental sharpness, and spiritual consciousness? If the answer is YES, then keep reading because healing has *already* begun. I commend you for the courage to face your own inner darkness, and I'm confident that you will find the light sooner than you think!

This book is dedicated to you and your journey of finding the healthiest, happiest and most impressive version of yourself. Healing will happen when you let it. Are you ready? If so, buckle up, because it may be a bumpy ride.

—Introduction—
Sophie's Story

Healing is on its way to you and, by taking one step at a time, you will someday look back and see how far you are from where your journey began.

In 1999, I was a college athlete, student, girlfriend and socially dynamic young woman, who lived every moment to the fullest. Since my main focus was social, academics and athletics took a back seat, and it became challenging to juggle all three. I had an enormous love for field hockey, which was a great release for the pent-up aggression I'd stored since childhood. The sport had taught me dedication, devotion and inspiration in the truest way, but college athletics was a whole different story.

I hadn't always been the athletic type in high school; actually, I'd been quite overweight. I called it "horizontally endowed" and "vertically challenged", but I carried it well. At one point, when I was only 5'2", I got on the scale and it said 200 pounds! The problem was, I was active in sports, had a strong appetite and always seemed to save more calories than I spent. But, after seeing the 200 pound mark on the scale, I woke up and began to monitor my eating habits and increase my workouts. I lost the first twenty pounds quite easily, and then seemed to drop the next thirty by going on radical diets. The last twenty-five pounds was another story.

As I went away to college for my freshman year, I carried those last twenty-five pounds along with all the other demands of being a college student. I tried to blend my academic, social, and weight loss goals, but became so overwhelmed that I turned to food in a dramatic and unhealthy way. At first, I avoided carbs during the week, binged on sweets each Saturday (to the point of sugar intoxication) and then wouldn't eat a morsel all day Sunday. I kept this schedule up for a couple of months, and even managed to lose weight. I got down to my goal weight, but little did I know what hitting my goal weight actually meant. When you lose weight, you unlock issues from the past that put the weight on in the first place and I was not yet ready to face the hidden issues that had been unlocked from my weight loss. That summer, I left a lot behind—my boyfriend, my ideal weight, my new college friends—and began to unconsciously slide into my personal demise.

When I returned to college for my sophomore year, I conditioned for field hockey, worried about academics, and used food abusively. By mid-season, the stress grew and I was no longer able to stick to *any* eating regimen. As a result, I found myself obsessively overeating every time I felt stressed. The guilt of eating was so unbearable that purging became a form of relief from the shame. At this point in my life, the emotions inside me were so extreme that I had no clue how to handle them. I didn't know who I was, nor did I know how to cope with the overwhelming anxiety and fear that I felt. So I ate excessive amounts of food and then I threw it up. This is when my binge/ purge relationship began.

I abused food, binged, felt overwhelmed with guilt, and then had to get what I'd eaten out of me. This cycle gave me a false feeling of control over my body and weight gain. Since I was never able to get all the food I consumed out of me, I was actually gaining weight. The guilt and shame I felt were so painful and immense that I began to struggle with getting through each day which, in turn, created more binges. It was like a vicious cycle that simply wouldn't end. I felt that there was no way out, and it kept me miserable and trapped in my own self-created hell. I wanted to die.

In addition to my food problems, I had begun some other bad habits: drinking to excess and using recreational drugs. Since I didn't understand how to manage my body, my emotions, my spirit, or my life in general, these chemical habits were causing an even bigger imbalance in my body and life.

In 2001, I decided to come home from school for the Easter weekend. I rarely went to church but, that Sunday, I did. The Easter sermon was about *The Start of New Beginnings*. That afternoon, I sat and talked with my mom on the porch. I had (and still have) a great relationship with my mom, and have always regarded her as both my rock and best friend. At this time in my life, binging and purging was my secret and I had never told a soul—not even her—about it. All of a sudden, I confessed that I had been throwing up my food. My secret—my abusive relationship with food—was revealed. I had gone out of my way to hide this from everyone for so long and, on Easter Sunday, I had verbally opened up about my self-abuse.

I believe that this is when a Divine Intervention began. That was one of the first miracles I saw God perform in my life. At the time, however, I thought, *"Oh no, my binging and purging secret has been revealed! Now what?"* I felt a profound confusion. I'd been brought out of the darkness and into the light, but now I felt exposed and unaware of what to do in that light. I'd been raised as a Christian and had been involved in church off and on all of my life, but now I was actually *experiencing* God.

It felt that something inside me knew that I was miserable and wanted to help! I had no idea how to get better and, with only three weeks of school left, I wanted to give up, come home and crash. My mom rejected this idea, and instead encouraged me to finish the semester. But she wisely gave me three conditions: she challenged me to not drink any alcohol, do any drugs, or purge for the rest of the semester. She said, "If you want to eat, eat, but keep the food down and stay away from the drugs." I agreed to this, and realized that I had made a very serious promise. I've always believed that the strongest thing you have is what you say so, by making a verbal agreement, I knew I would honor it to its fullest.

With the new concept of allowing myself to overeat but then not throw it up, I began to quickly see the reality of what overeating does to the body. My Easter confession to and challenge from my mom led me to make a commitment, which ultimately saved my life. I truly felt that God had stepped in and was introducing me to the next phase of my life, which would be all about **healing**.

I went back to school and had a difficult time. I binged (but wouldn't purge), dealt with many strong and confusing emotions, felt overwhelmed, but followed the commitment I made to my mom to abstain from alcohol, drugs and throwing up my food. I was sober and, when I binged, I felt miserable.

It was the biggest party week of the school year and I was sober, which helped me see things in a way I'd never seen before. I went to parties, stayed out late, was the designated driver and remained true to my promise of sobriety until the semester was over. I tried to straddle two different worlds—health and parties—which was difficult while living in an unbalanced frame of mind, but was ultimately the overlap that changed my life forever.

Toward the end of that next week, the parties were starting earlier and ending later. One Saturday, I spent the day listening to live Reggae and dancing at a nearby party. I had walked upstairs to use the bathroom and a girl who lived across the hall from me, Sara, was waiting in line as well. She was leaning against the wall and the light was shining through a curtain, creating a soft glow around her face. With her head rested against the wall, she began to sing. She had an incredible voice and sounded like an angel! She was obviously intoxicated, but there was something spiritual about that moment. That evening, I was driving a whole crew of drunk people around, and we ended up at a bar downtown. I can remember looking across the bar that night and seeing Sara again. Little did I know that it would be the last time I'd ever see her alive.

Early that next morning, I received the news that Sara had been killed in a drunken driving accident. The pain and shock I felt when learning of her death showed me the severity of our choices and where they can lead. That incident changed my life forever. I can remember sitting at her funeral and feeling as if a part of me had died with her: the part of me that was already killing myself. I returned home for the summer, deciding that my time at that college was over, and realized that it was time to deal with my issues.

If there is a positive side to having a food addiction, it's that there's an immediate consequence, such as weight gain, which can really get your attention to show you that there actually is an imbalance in your life. After I stopped throwing up my food, I was still consuming far more calories than my body needed and, consequently I gained a lot of weight. The extra pounds really were alarming, but I still didn't know what to do about it.

That fall, everything came crashing down on me. One Saturday night, I sat on our couch at home crying to my mom. I simply didn't want to live anymore. The pain of life felt unbearable and I wanted it all to be over. Her words pierced my heart forever. "Sophie," she said, "I think it is time for you to visit your spiritual side again." After hearing that, for the first time in a long time, I felt a glimpse of hope. That night, I called out to God, Spirit, The Creator, or anything that would listen and said, "God, if you are really out there, please save me."

The next morning I was invited to church and went, but did so unenthusiastically. At first, I had no idea what I was about to search for and find, but I knew that I was ready. The pain of staying in the present was so overwhelming that I was ready—with all the courage in the world—to embrace the unknown. This is when my healing really began to transform me. I felt like a drained battery that was finally plugged in and able to recharge. I knew in my heart that spirituality was an essential piece to this healing puzzle and, as I let God into my body, emotions, mind, and soul, my life slowly began to change.

Early on in my healing process, I was shown that there were four pieces to work on to complete the picture of health: the body, emotions, mind, and spirit. In retrospect, I now realize that I was limited because I didn't understand how to keep the four components working together and at their optimum!

Over the next ten years, I dug through all my dark inner issues and eventually found healing. Now I understand that healing is a pretty word that has an ugly process. My healing took place **one awareness at a time**, and I began to understand that all the things that had hurt me so bad in my past had appeared in order to teach me great life lessons.

I began to face the things I had run from and soon learned that, when you look into this inner darkness with God on your side, it becomes an illusion of a shadow that evaporates into thin air. In the long run, all the thoughts and feelings that I never knew what to do with (or how to process) began to have a purpose. Through this long journey of healing, the belief that **everything in life happens for a reason** was born.

Over time, I recognized that I was actually comfortable living with problems and pain. I only knew how to experience life through difficulties and this was the foundation for my struggle with food. Peaceful living had never been part of my awareness but, once I had this insight, I was able to look at each day's challenges in a different way. Fortunately, my compulsive overeating ended up being the teacher which ultimately led me to find greater awareness and discover ways to live life to the fullest.

The road I traveled led me right into God's lap, which is where I was able to truly know myself and understand the abundance of all that life is. I learned what health honestly means and found love in ways I never knew existed. Peace introduced itself to me through acceptance of each moment, deep breaths, and trust. As I look back at my journey, I can see the abundance of lessons, which I initially perceived as trials but which turned out to be blessings.

Today, I practice being centered within, so that no matter what is happening on the outside, I'm able to embrace and honor being okay. Each day, I work to keep my body, emotions, mind, and spirit in a balanced place so I can continue to learn more about myself, what my purpose is, and—most important—how to manifest love.

For a very long time, I felt an inner voice encouraging me to share my story and all the techniques that changed my life. I just knew that others were also struggling with this same issue of self-demise, and some of the things that were transformational to me might be helpful to them as well. Fortunately, healing can be an incredible and rewarding process that introduces you to your true self. Transformation is available to all of us, and this book is dedicated to you on your own journey of finding freedom, happiness, laughter, love, trust and wisdom.

I know that everything happens for a reason and, right now, you are in your perfect place. My hope is that this book activates your courage within to uncover the healthiest, happiest and most impressive version of yourself. Healing is on its way to you and, by taking one step at a time, you will—like me—someday look back and see how far you are from where your journey began.

Sophie

—PART ONE—

Facing Your Issues with Food

—Chapter 1—
Food Isn't the Problem

*Transforming the continuous appetite is a process of looking
within to discover what's happening underneath the craving.*

If food is for fuel, then why do we have taste buds? All humans
must eat to survive—without exceptions—and, if we didn't have
taste buds, we might not have the drive to eat. The purpose of eating,
however, has become so tangled into a web of tasting rather than fueling
that people are getting increasingly imbalanced with every passing bite.

I like to call out-of-control taste buds "cravings". These little guys
are important and serve us in many ways. At times (when our inner
issues surface), they can take over and cause us to feel uncomfortable.
If you have a craving right now, I challenge you to first recognize that
something is going on in your inner life, and the coping mechanism
you've chosen is food. The problem, however, is not food; it's rather the
"result" from an unacknowledged problem in your life. In the past, these

inner issues have probably caused outrageous cravings that have made you feel bad, but the way out is near. These harmful cravings are called **the continuous appetite.**

Have you ever used food to comfort your **body** in a time of need or perhaps as a form of stress relief at the end of the day, even though it interferes with your weight loss or fitness goals? If so, you are familiar with how your **body's** cravings can result in self-sabotage caused by **the continuous appetite**.

Have you ever been in a great mood **emotionally** and then—all of a sudden—a co-worker made a comment or your spouse gave you a look, and you immediately felt horrible? This nasty feeling then sends you frantically to the fridge, throwing your weight-loss goals out the window. This is how a lack of emotional awareness stimulates **the continuous appetite**.

Do you ever get stuck inside your **mind** with thoughts like, *"What should I eat? What should I order? Why do I have to struggle with food on a daily basis?"* If so, these are the thoughts the mind will generate when something is out of balance within. The damaging result is the breakdown of the **mind**, which then speaks the language of **the continuous appetite**.

Have you ever felt empty and disconnected from life and asked yourself, *"What is the point anyway, who cares – nothing matters…"*? This is how inner **spiritual** emptiness uses a facade that feels like hunger but, instead, actually activates **the continuous appetite**.

If any of these scenarios seem and sound familiar, you're not alone. I have lived through this darkness and, at times, thought I wouldn't make it. But I've overcome these obstacles and, if I did it, you can too! All these negative experiences that happen in the **body, emotions, mind and spirit**, (or your **BEMS**) will be your key to unlocking true freedom from continuous eating. Our relationship with food is something that we all have to address every day and, when you struggle with this issue, it can seem as if life is overwhelming. There is a way out, however, from the body's cravings, emotional dysfunction, mental chatter and spiritual emptiness which are the ultimate roots of your intense cravings—and that way out is **awareness.**

Awareness will be the light that leads you out of the darkness, but we can't shine all of it on you at once. We need to gradually introduce you to it like a gentle sunrise, so you have time to adjust to the radiance. The exercises and techniques offered in this book can be thought of as mini beams of light that will shine through your darkness. Naturally, the more you practice, the brighter you will become.

The first step is to examine the relationship you currently have with what you eat. Take a look at where you currently stand with food because the first step to changing any behavior is identification. I want you to think about your relationship with eating as if it were a person, and then answer these questions:

- *How do I act around food?*
- *What makes me cheat on my goals?*
- *Where do I tend to overdo it?*
- *How do I obsess over it?*
- *When do I sneak it?*

Your answers will shed some light on your relationship with food, which will bring awareness and, through awareness, you will be shown in which way you need to grow.

Inner Issues Beneath Overeating

We all have issues—big ones, small ones, obvious ones, and even invisible ones—and no one is issue-free. I don't care who you are, how much you have or don't have; not one of us is impervious to or exempt from having issues. Everyone on Earth has some kind of issue, and there are statistics that classify up to 85% of families in America as "dysfunctional". So having life conflicts has practically become the American standard but, when we try to ignore our issues, they turn into problems or cravings. When we unconsciously react to our problems by acting on our cravings, we create even more inner dysfunction.

We do, however, have a choice, and making this choice is crucial if we want to heal **the continuous appetite**. The necessary decision is to begin facing our true inner issues. Life offers all of us information and messages beyond the surface of each life situation. When we don't hear (or listen to) the message being presented, a problem can turn into a dilemma. When we don't tackle the dilemma, it turns into a calamity and, when the calamity is left unresolved, our life becomes steeped in turmoil.

I knew that place of turmoil well. I used to live there, and wondered why my life always seemed so troubled. I would encounter problem after problem and craving after craving, steeped in my own self-generated turmoil. But once I began to work through some of my issues, I started to see that these situations had presented themselves long before I became consciously aware of them. This taught me that I could now begin to be more conscious and avoid living in the turmoil. I then moved to the level of the problems and began to analyze those, which led me to the awareness that each problem—at one point—was a message. My goal then became to live on the level of information and messages. That's when I learned how peaceful life can be when I make decisions to look in a different direction and ask new questions.

I had been so out of balance in my body, emotions, mind, and spirit that my mind had convinced me that food and cravings were my problem. But then I began to see that the problem was a lack of being able to deal with what was happening in my life.

Up until this point, you too may have focused on diets, exercises and rules to change your issues with food or cravings. The dilemma, however, doesn't exist in the food. It lives in the imbalance of your four components; the **body, emotions, mind, and spirit**. I can't emphasize strongly enough how important these four components are and, when out of balance, how much inner suffering (disguised as the coping mechanism of overeating) they can cause. Once you stop regarding food as the problem and begin to look deeper and start **seeing your cravings as the messenger**, you will heal the real issues inside, which are the cause of **the continuous appetite**. The good news is that, once you're ready to look within, you will begin to transform this dreadful habit and so much more!

The Difference Between a Craving and Hunger

We all know the sounds and the feeling of hunger: the thunderous roar from the belly, the weakness that emerges right before lunch, or the watergates of a salivating mouth when the aroma of food passes by. A craving can feel very similar but, rather than a thunderous roar from the belly, it is more like a **bodily** need to be with that food immediately. This may manifest as a watering mouth triggered by an **emotional** attachment to a specific food, a re-occurring picture in your **mind** of a precise food, or quite simply as the experience of deep inner **spiritual** hunger that no food can even touch.

Hunger and cravings can seem similar but they are, in fact, worlds apart! Stated simply, **hunger is the simple need to eat in order to fuel the body so it can function optimally**, while **a craving is an immediate need or desire for a specific food to "satisfy" something.**

Do you know the difference between your feelings of hunger and cravings? When you're not clear about what is going on **within your *inner life*,** hunger can manifest as a craving and cravings as hunger. **Acting** on a craving, however, is a fruitless behavior because it's prompted by a deep issue within, an issue from which food can't even provide relief.

5

I once had a client who really struggled with recognizing the difference between hunger and cravings and, as a result, she became very defensive about her food cravings. She would say things like, "I just want chocolate, and chocolate is all that I want." I would ask her to look deeper into what the chocolate made her **feel** like or what the chocolate **gave** her.

Eventually, she opened up to herself, overcame her old resistance, and discovered that chocolate made her feel relaxed. She would suck on chocolate, and this act was both comforting and nurturing to her. We then realized that this instinct to suck was much more than a need for chocolate; it was an inner need to feel soothed, comforted and nurtured and, for her, chocolate had become the way for her to touch those feelings. But, because she was using food to medicate her emotional self, the good feelings couldn't be sustained. As a result, she would need to eat more and more chocolate. Once we recognized what she really was craving, we were able to break the cycle of eating and find other ways in which she could achieve the needed feelings of being relaxed, nurtured and comforted.

When the body is low on energy, you need to give it fuel but, when the body is **craving** something, it means it's time to look within and investigate what else might be going on. (Now, this doesn't mean that you can never have food that you innocently crave; it just means you're willing to look deeper before taking that first bite.) Challenge your cravings. Remember, cravings can never be satisfied; they just change from one desire to the next. The only true way to find real relief from a craving is to look within and conduct an inner investigation to discover exactly what the message behind the craving is. Only you can identify the difference between your hunger and cravings, but knowing the difference and then learning how to tune into your body is the beginning of unlocking **the continuous appetite**.

Holistic Harmony

The term *"holistic"* means to view the whole system rather than the individual parts. When you look at your "holistic" self, you can see how the four components of the self (**the BEMS: body, emotions, mind and spirit**) affect one another. Let's take the idea of hunger. This is a reflex that our body intelligently uses to keep us alive. It first appears as a **feeling** in the **body** before it then stimulates **thought**, which creates the **action** of getting food to fulfill the request. Every component affects the other, and most life situations follow this same subconscious sequence.

When your four basic components are out of balance, you will notice excessive—inner and outer—conflict in your life. These imbalances will appear through continuous eating, but what is really happening is an inability to deal with anxiety, fear, or just plain unhappiness. When your vital components (BEMS) are functioning at an optimal level, however, the self (or inner you) is balanced and the outer dysfunction begins to fade away. As you begin to explore your inner life, remember that it's important to look at all the different parts of yourself—**body, emotions, mind, and spirit**—and evaluate how (and to what extent) they may be out of balance.

The BODY's Brilliance

Your body is made up of countless molecules. One molecule holds enough information to fill four hundred books as thick as the bible. Our bodies are amazing machines and are more reliable than anything man has to offer. One person contains up to 75 billion cells. Although these cells are microscopic, they are what keep us functioning on a healthy and balanced level. They're our friends but, most of the time, we don't take enough time to sit back and realize the miracle that's taking place behind the scenes. Every single cell lives in a tiny pouch of water which acts as a blanket around the cell. So, if a person is dehydrated, every cell is being denied its proper environment to function optimally.

I guarantee that you already know what is best for your body. Everyone knows what it means to be healthy. This might include being hydrated, in sound physical shape, nutritionally balanced, and well-rested. When you place your body under healthy circumstances, it generally responds beautifully. There are so many different approaches to physical health out there that I encourage you to research and find what feels right to you, and concentrate on one at a time. Begin doing one good thing for your body today, and watch how it grows into a new, healthy habit. Starting with one thing at a time gives you the endurance to do two things that are good for you by next week and, before you know it, you'll be living a life of complete well-being within a year!

Being EMOTIONALLY Balanced

Having emotional balance is not about being happy. Instead, it's about being in touch with the current emotion you are feeling, whether it feels good or not, and then knowing what to do with that understanding. Often, anger, anxiety, depression, fear, frustration, irritation, and/or struggle are signs that something is internally out of harmony. When you feel these emotions, *really* feel them! It is okay to feel, and no one can ever tell you that you don't feel something. The goal, however, is to be closely in touch with your emotions and then know how to handle them most effectively when they do surface.

When an emotion confronts us, it's easy to look outside ourselves and say, "She hurt me." But I encourage you instead to take responsibility for your own emotional experience. Something may have just happened on the outside that triggered an emotion within you, but it's important to remember that this emotion is in YOU. It's not someone else's fault for touching it.

When you identify what's going on in you emotionally, you will discover the power of being emotionally aware. First, ask yourself the following questions when you think you may need an emotional tune-up:

- *What emotion am I feeling?*
- *How does this emotion make me feel?*
- *When have I felt this emotion before?*

Asking these three questions will help you begin to build your emotional understanding. Remember, the way to change is by welcoming new consciousness, allowing answers to come to the surface, and then trusting the discoveries you make.

Silencing the MIND's Chatter

The mind is like a garden. When the chatter is weeded out and the cognition is fed (as with water and sunlight) the now (or present moment) will blossom. What are you thinking about right now? Are you even aware of your thought patterns? Researchers say we have about 60,000 thoughts a day, which is a lot to keep up with. Out of all your various thoughts, how many of them are productive and how many are meaningless?

When your thoughts are meaningless, full of static, and out of control, we call this *chatter.* Chatter is like a stream of random sentences that don't connect to one another, producing constant high-volume babble. *"Did I do the laundry?" "Oh I forgot to go to the store!" "I like her outfit..."* etc. Unfortunately, this is the type of information that is processed on the level of chatter, and this **will not help you.** Instead of helping you be more productive or efficient, it actually takes you out of the moment and lures you into even more meaningless chatter.

If we continue the analogy of the mind being like a garden, chatter then is like a weed growing in your mind. What do weeds do? They steal all the nutrients from the soil that would promote a healthy garden! In order to become the true master of your own mind, it's essential to learn how to silence the chatter. The first step is to recognize when your mind is full of chatter, and the second step is to consciously silence it by flipping the switch.

Let's draw a picture. Imagine that there are many people gathered around a painting at a museum, and all of them are waiting to hear the artist speak about his work. Eventually, everyone flocks together and the gallery attendant tries to silence the audience by quietly saying, "Ok, the artist is ready to speak." But the mumble in the audience continues, because no one has responded to the attendant. The frustrated artist then assertively steps in and says, "Shush!" The audience pauses, then grows quiet and, at this point, the artist finally has the audience's full attention and respect. Chatter-filled minds will respond this same way to a passionate *"Shush!"*

This continuous and repetitive practice will take time to master, but it will dramatically change—and enhance—the power you have in your mind. We will expand upon this concept later in the book but, for now, **just focus on learning how to recognize the chatter and then silence it!** Just remember—whenever needed—to give it a quick, strong, non-verbal *"Shush!"*

Developing SPIRITUAL Consciousness

Spiritual consciousness is the idea of connecting to God, Spirit, a Higher Power or something greater than a human in order to achieve an inner sense of peace and belonging. The name or language that you use to describe this relationship is not important; what is important is the faith that's required to have such a connection. We all have a place in us that is empty, and the only thing that can really fill it up is an unworldly, divine connection with God.

Being connected to all-powerful and present God, is an invisible gift that's available to us on a daily basis. God exists in the now but, when we are caught up in distracting and destructive chatter, it's hard to experience a spiritual presence. Whether you need to reestablish a former connection or find a new one, what's important is creating a bond and union with a power greater than yourself. This is one of the greatest steps that I took toward my own healing, and I know that, when you invite God into your life, God shows up.

Once you get in touch with the four levels of yourself (your BEMS), over time, you will notice less conflict, diminished drama, and you will be more wholly available to the people in your life. This is because taking the time to know what is happening on the inside helps you begin to better know how to handle what's going on outside.

Your Holistic Tool Box

The *Holistic Tool box* is the idea of creating a storage center which holds all the exercises, ideas, techniques, and tips you've collected throughout the book. The idea of creating an inspirational tool box came from my own journey. I would write down and decorate meaningful sayings and collect many insights that were significant to me along my journey. I then noticed that I had accumulated a lot of great stuff in my journal, my "tool box" at the time, and it became like an emergency kit that I ran to whenever one of life's challenges surfaced. That's why I named it my *"Holistic Tool Box"*. It can be an actual box, a journal, or even a file on your computer. The idea is to store all the instruction, information, and guidance you've resonated with—in one space—for future use. You can be as creative or technical as you want, but it's a great reference center for you when you run into the fluctuations of life.

When you find something to be effective and/or helpful as you break through your barriers and inner issues, place it in your holistic tool box. An example of things you may want to put into your tool box would be a meaningful article you read, an inspiring quote you came across, a photo from a magazine that gave you a positive feeling, or even a page from your own journal where you walked yourself through a difficult situation. Of course, not everything works equally well for everyone, which is why your *Holistic Tool Box* is specifically important to you, and you alone. It's a great way to keep suggestions for your future self about what you can do if you happen to run into a craving or challenging situation.

Resistance to the Journal

When I first began journaling, I really didn't see the point. I thought, *"So I am supposed to open a book and write? How will this be helpful?"* At the time I didn't realize that journaling was like an emotional, mental, and spiritual bathroom break. Your mind can use journaling as a wise removal system to get rid of what you no longer need or use, and you can thus release the unusable, toxic emotional/ mental waste matter left over from the day before.

Elimination is the way your body journals. Similarly, the **emotions, mind, and spirit** need to eliminate the toxic waste matter left over from yesterday. I encourage you to drop your resistance to journaling and give it a try. Make an effort to thoughtfully journal for seven days in a row, five minutes at a time. If you do not see a positive result, you can stop, but it's crucial to release your resistance and see what all this journaling fuss is about.

So many people are scared to journal because they are afraid. *"What if somebody reads this,"* they think, or even worse, *"What if the person it is about, reads it?"* This is the standard fear that people have when it comes to journaling and I have a suggestion on this topic.

Get a spiral notebook from the store—one that you are not afraid to tear apart and throw away. So many people buy beautiful journals, but then find it hard to truly unleash the inner garbage because they feel their journal is indispensable and fear someone will look inside. To avoid this stutter, buy a spiral notebook once per month, throwing each used one away at the end of each month. If that does not feel secure enough, journal on a piece of paper, tear it out, and then throw it away in a public trash can. Or, if you still fear your words are not private, tear the paper into pieces and throw it away, then pour ketchup on it. The whole point is to get it out and not hold onto it anymore.

In this book, I will ask you to journal about many different things and will give you specific questions to answer and truly encourage you to do the journaling assignment. Journaling is a calm and wise way to let go of your past issues, and serves as a "trash can" of sorts, where you can throw out your chatter, ideas, thoughts, and all the mental, emotional, and spiritual garbage that is causing your cravings. Try to not obsess about your handwriting, grammar, spelling, or sentence structure. Just let out whatever is on your mind. These assignments are what changed my life and they can have a transformational impact on yours as well!

Life will continuously provide you with ups and downs, so the more tools you have stored away at your disposal, the better able you will be to face what surfaces. Transforming **the continuous appetite** is a process of looking within to discover what's happening underneath the craving.

The Daily Basics

This exercise is to be done on a daily basis. Just as you would take a shower every day, *The Daily Basics* are the way to clean your BEMS from the inner gunk you no longer need. Please find a safe and quiet place where you can sit down for about 20 minutes with little or no interruption.

A. *Get a journal, set a timer for five minutes and write about whatever is on your mind.*

B. *Then, answer these questions in your journal to tune into yourself—Inner Refresher Questions:*

1. *What sensations do I feel in my body today?*

2. *What am I feeling right now?*

3. *What am I thinking about?*

4. *What does my spiritual connection feel like today?*

C. *Next, make a list of five things you are thankful for, with no repeats!*

D. *Finally, quiet your mind, and sit in silence for ten minutes.*

If you found this exercise to be helpful, please store it in your *Holistic Tool Box.*

Chapter 2

I Just Ate Too Much

Looking at what is underneath the continuous appetite is the immediate entry into unlocking your inner issues and unveiling your true self.

C arol is 32 years old, has an average build, is attractive, and most people who look at her would never know that she needs to lose weight. Carol, however, has a struggle going on behind the scenes, a battle which the naked eye can't see. She's in a constant state of fighting against herself, her body, her weight and everything she puts into her mouth. She has severe issues with overeating and feeling guilt, and then beating herself up, and (sometimes) even binging and purging.

One night, Carol gets home late after a company kickball game. She has not eaten much today, (out of guilt from the frappuccino she drank earlier in the day, rationalizing that it was at least half of her daily calories), so she chooses to skip eating dinner before the game. Now, she is home, tired, starving and prowling around the kitchen.

She decides to eat a piece of fruit, under the assumption that it is the extent of the permissible calories she has left for the day. So she eats some plump cherries that are in season and then, all of a sudden, Carol finds herself obsessively shoving popcorn, chips, cookies, and anything bite-size, into her mouth. In the moment, thoughts go by like, *"Carol, stop doing this, you're going to regret it."* But she continues shoveling the food into her mouth and, before long, she realizes that she has just entered **the continuous eating zone** and a wave of self-disgust overwhelms her.

Have you ever found yourself in Carol's shoes? Eating and eating and eating and, even though you know that you won't be happy with this choice later, you're unable to stop? Once the eating has ended, it's as if a wave of self-hatred hits you in the face and begins to drown you. This wave has a crashing that sounds like—*"I'm a failure, I can't accomplish the goals I set, I'm not good enough, I can't ever say no, I can't, can't, can't..."* This is the wave of self-disgust that comes after continuous eating. But, rather than continuing to let this wave hit you in the face, let's learn how to surf.

The ocean represents your life. The waves are the constant changes that life offers. The surfer is you, and the surfboard is the sum of tools you will collect through this book. The first step is to remember that **food is not the problem**. Instead, food is the foam from a wave—simply a distraction. The next step is to begin to see how all the waves of life affect you, and then learn to deal with them differently. The final step is using the tools in this book to get up on your board and surf the waves of life.

Ate Too Much?

So you just overate. Stop whatever you are doing, wherever you are. Get out of that room, go as far as 30 to 50 feet away and as you are leaving, grab three things: chewing gum, your journal, and water. Getting out of that physical space will reduce the continuous flow of counterproductive energy that you're both surrounded by and emitting. Once you are physically out of the area, you will find that the emotional intensity will diminish, even if you're still chewing the food.

You grabbed three things: chewing gum, your journal, and water. The point of the gum is to release tension that may just exist in the jaw and simply needs a release. The point of journaling is to get the body to release the emotional, mental, and spiritual gunk from your system. It is like a bathroom break for your emotions, mind, and spirit; it can be very refreshing. The water's purpose is to drink and begin to hydrate yourself since cravings can originate from dehydration.

Now breathe and come back to yourself and the moment. Look around and see that everything is okay right now. If anything doesn't feel okay, it's just a thought, and you may need to do some detective work to see if that thought is merely chatter. If so, silence it.

The Four Questions

In your journal, you can begin to face yourself on a deeper level by answering *The Four Questions.* These questions (which are referred to throughout the book) will help you reflect and develop some insight into what is going on underneath your eating and cravings. After you have fled the scene of **the continuous eating zone**, chewed gum, opened your journal, and drunk water; it's time to tap into your inner life and explore yourself.

Question One:
What happened today?

This question will help you stop and reflect back on **what happened in your day**. Sometimes we can have experiences, feelings or thoughts that trigger us and we don't even know it's happening. This first question will help you reflect upon your day and see what happened that might have knocked you off balance and caused the subsequent overeating reaction. When asked the question **"What happened today?"**, your response might be, "I used up my calories and didn't have any left for dinner. I really want to lose weight, which is why I am having so few calories, but I figured I didn't have enough daily calories left for dinner. What I'm noticing is that, **when I tell myself that I'm not able to eat or give myself dinner, I always seem to end up overeating at night.**"

Question Two:
What emotion am I feeling?

This question takes you one step further into yourself. We can get so out of touch with what is going on emotionally that we subconsciously create coping mechanisms to counter-balance this emotional unawareness. Then, we may even think that life and outer circumstances have caused the imbalance within. But the truth of the matter is that the imbalance was only triggered by something that exists inside. By asking this question, you will begin to get in touch with **what is going on emotionally**. You might ask yourself, *"What emotion am I feeling?"* And your answer might be, *"I was hungry, and angry that I wouldn't allow to myself eat. I didn't realize it at the time, but the thought that I can't eat or have dinner makes me so mad. Why can't I have dinner? I just want to be normal and I'm angry that I have to fight myself every day. So **I guess I was feeling angry, resentful, anxious, and bitter and, when I feel those feelings, I usually push them down with food.**"*

Question Three:
What does that emotion feel like within?

This next question will help you identify **how** these emotions are being played out. Answer this question with the intention of describing how the feelings feel. What does the anger, resentment, anxiety and bitterness feel like? You might find yourself admitting, *"It feels horrible. It makes me want to run away, or punch something. It feels like fire, fear, and panic all at once. I can't handle that knot of feelings, so I've learned to shut them up with food. **After I eat, I feel so bad about myself but, for some reason, I can deal with those bad feelings over the other feelings."***

Question Four:
What do I want to feel?

Up to this point, you have probably thought that what you wanted was food but, if so, why is it so hard to stop eating, and why can you never get enough food? The answer is because the food is not what you truly want. What you truly want is something that you can't eat or taste. It's usually something you want to feel or experience, and it's buried deep within. But asking this question will help you uncover what it is that you truly want. Most people aren't in touch with what they truly want but are in touch with what they don't want, and being informed only about what you don't want keeps you right where you don't want to be. This question is here to help you look in a different direction and discover what it is you're truly looking for. Stop and think for a moment. Ask yourself: Do you want to feel better about yourself? Do you want to feel loved and accepted? Do you want to be happy and not struggle with life so much? If this is what you want, you must first discover **what** is causing you to keep using food to fill this hole. If you want to be happy and feel loved, you must first uncover **the reason** you keep running to food, which only leaves you feeling bad and hated. If you want to be accepted, there is first a need to practice feeling better about yourself, and accept that food has nothing to do with this. A vital step toward beginning to love and accept yourself is to ask yourself, *"So what is causing me to keep eating?"* Ok, so now I see that food can't give me what I really want, so how do I get self-love and acceptance? If you can ask yourself these brave questions, then congratulations! You are now asking the right questions that will empower you! And, as you continue to read on, you will learn how to find and uncover the secrets to practicing self-love and acceptance.

These four questions changed my life, and I encourage you to practice them the second you realize you're in **the continuous eating zone**. As you write out your answers, you will go deeper into yourself and see what needs to heal. It may seem scary at first, but I assure you it will free you from the prison of overeating.

The Familiar Zones

After you recognize that overeating is just a coping mechanism created to fill up a bigger hole within, you will come to realize that this hole will never be satisfied with food because the hole has nothing to do with food. Instead, it probably has to do with an inner emptiness that needs healing.

Eating has become a way to not deal with whatever is happening within you, deep down, and your "familiar" has become what you know. You may have become so familiar (even comfortable) with the bad feelings that arrive after you overeat that you subconsciously choose to overeat because those feelings are easier to handle than the true knot of emotion within, which has *trained* you to eat in the first place.

The feelings underneath, which cause your cravings, are what we need to address. You may not be fond of the idea that you have familiar zones and that these zones feel terrible, but this is the beginning of an opportunity for you to see how powerful you really are. This is a chance for you to see that at some point you made a decision to be a survivor. When you get to the point of surviving, your decisions (or coping mechanisms) then typically come from a place of desperation and not from conscious thought. You are then left reacting rather than acting. But that's okay because, through reading this book (and doing the exercises), you are going to unlock yourself from the prison of overeating.

Now is the time to begin making different choices. You're at this place in your life because of the decisions you made up to this point but, if you want a different future or better "familiar zones", you need to be open to trying different things. Right now, I ask you to make a different, healthier choice to face the unknown feelings, thoughts or circumstances in you, instead of pushing them down with food. You may not yet be aware of what is happening that causes you to overeat but, when you start to ask *The Four Questions*, you will easily unlock essential information that will help you transform your food cravings.

Awareness is the Master Key

Consciousness. Knowledge. Mindfulness. Understanding. What do these terms have in common? They are all synonyms for awareness. Awareness is the master key that will assist you in your self-healing journey. Awareness is an interesting process which unfolds naturally in its own time and, when you make awareness a goal, you will observe fascinating characteristics within the waves of life.

The process of awareness goes like this: first, you become aware *after* you do something, then you're aware *while* you're doing it, then you become aware right *before* you do it, then you gain awareness that you *might do it soon,* then you become so aware that you *stop doing* that thing. Right now, you're aware that you don't want to continuously overeat; soon you'll be aware before you do it. This will happen through being conscious, mindful, and more aware of your BEMS (body, emotions, mind, and spirit) on a daily basis.

Awareness of Your Body

Your body is always working for you and it does a great job. When was the last time you had to remind your eyes to blink, your heart to beat, your stomach to digest, or your kidneys to function? Probably not recently. We spend so much time judging and hating our bodies when, in fact, they really are magical machines. All your body is trying to do for you is balance all the demands you put on it.

Your body is an immaculate machine that is designed to heal itself when placed in the right circumstances. Therefore, if something is out of whack, instead of getting mad at the body, you can look at what the body is trying to communicate to you. For example, if you are gaining weight, having pain, or experiencing an annoying symptom, there is an imbalance that needs to be addressed.

Look for (and find) all the things that your body does for you. Pay attention to how it recovers, heals sores, restores what is broken, and—naturally—brings you back into a state of balance. Practice thankfulness for your body, and become aware of its wholeness. This shift in your attitude will restore your body's ability to be healthy!

Emotional Awareness

Getting in touch with your emotions is like growing a tree. Can you just plant the seed, pour water on it and expect to see a full grown tree? No. It takes time for the seed to unfold into its fullest potential. The tree knows all along what its destiny is but needs time to grow, branch by branch, leaf by leaf and season by season. The same thing will happen as you begin to ask yourself what you are truly experiencing and feeling. Asking yourself and going through *The Four Questions* will help you gain emotional awareness anytime you feel a little off or imbalanced.

Mental Awareness

Are you in touch with your thoughts? Now that you have been working on silencing the chatter, I want you to move to the next level of the mind: the thinking process. The sole purpose of cognition is to find solutions and, if you can't find solutions, it may be because your chatter is simply too loud. So remember to silence the chatter and allow your brain to become more peaceful.

When your brain is at peace, it acquires knowledge through thinking. Thinking can happen both consciously and subconsciously and sometimes your subconscious thoughts can create feelings that disempower you. So your first step is **to get in touch with what your mind is doing.**

The next step is to recognize your thoughts, check in with them and remember that you are the leader of your mind. Check in with yourself just like you would an old friend. Ask yourself how you are doing and what you are thinking about or experiencing. **Check in with yourself to help stop the chatter because, when the chatter is quiet, your behavior will change.**

This is a simple process that only requires memory and willingness. While it may be uncomplicated, it takes willingness and repetition to see the results that will empower you. Over time, as you practice this on a daily basis, you'll notice what your mind is doing **before** your actions show you. The whole process of healing is like being a detective. At this point, you know the crime (overeating) and, throughout this book, we will be back-tracking together in order to find the culprit or your inner issues.

Spiritual Awareness

If you were coming down with a cold and wanted to take Vitamin C, would you just take one pill? No. You'd take proper doses of it throughout the day and week in order to build a positive vitamin defense in your body to fight against destructive agents. Connecting spiritually follows the same principle. In order to stay healthy, you need to take a normal daily dose and, when life becomes out of balance because of outer circumstances, you'll need mega doses of spiritual connection to help get you through the situation.

An analogy that I have used to describe our human ability to have a spiritual connection is the image of a lamp. You are the lamp and you have a power cord. A lamp can sit on a table and be a lamp, whether it's turned on or not. But the purpose of a lamp is to provide light. In order for the lamp to shine, it needs to be plugged into a source of electricity and, once it is plugged in, the lamp will shine light and be at its fullest potential.

In this analogy, we (humans) are the lamp and God is the electricity that allows the lamp to shine. God is the source that provides energy so we can live our best life. We have this opportunity, therefore, to learn how to "plug into God" on a daily basis so we can shine our brightest. The language that I'll use to describe God in this book will fluctuate. It doesn't matter the way that God has shown up in your life or the language you use to describe this experience, or what religion you may follow or whether you follow one at all. What is important to me is that you make sure to connect on a daily basis to the magnificent source of energy that is larger than yourself. I encourage you to find the language that feels right to you and then insert **that** word anytime we talk about God.

You know what works for you. I can give you suggestions on how to pray or meditate (and later on in the book I will) but, right here and now, I want you to just take a moment and look at your current spiritual relationship. How does it need to grow, expand, or be more active? Trust whatever comes up and then make a commitment to connect to God for a couple of minutes per day, every day, before you get too busy and forget.

Activating your spiritual connection will help you be able to fuse with spiritual strength, combat your human weaknesses, and empower you to transform **the continuous appetite.**

When you follow the many suggestions on how to get in touch with the four areas of yourself (**the body, emotions, mind, and spirit**), I promise your awareness will grow and your cravings will fade. Looking at what is underneath **the continuous appetite** is the immediate entry into unlocking your inner issues and unveiling your true self.

—Inner-Query Two—

The Four Questions

These questions are the key to healing **the continuous appetite** and will be referred to often throughout the book. Drink these up like water. Get a 3x5 card out and write down these questions. Then place it in your purse, wallet, pocket or glove compartment. The key is to have it on you, so you can begin to check within and find out what is happening on the inside when you want to eat, feel a craving coming on, or simply want to be more aware.

    A. *Whenever you are unsure about why you want to eat, confused about what you might be feeling, going through, or thinking, please ask yourself The Four Questions:*

        1. *What happened today?*

        2. *What emotion was I feeling?*

        3. *What does this feel like within?*

        4. *What do I want to feel?*

            If you found this exercise to be helpful,
            please store it in your *Holistic Tool Box*.

—Chapter 3—
Preventing Overeating

Choosing thoughts that feel good will begin to help you disengage from the continuous appetite and connect you to your best self.

As I was going through my healing process, I heard countless people say, "Once you have an eating disorder, you'll always struggle with food—to some extent—for the rest of your life." That statement felt like finger nails down a chalkboard to me. I thought, *"If I have to wage a war with food and eating and do so three times a day for the rest of my life, I don't even want to live."* To me, this idea was cancerous. After much agony and anguish over that concept, the idea that came to me was, *"If I overcome and heal my own issues with food, I will write a book to help others heal and unlock all their issues as well."*

So here I am, **healed and healthy ten years later** and, if it can happen for me, it can happen for you too! You CAN heal and overcome your issues with food, 100%, regardless of the severity of your issues.

I'm here to discredit the idea that you must struggle with this problem forever. The reason some people do struggle with food and cravings "for life" is because they **haven't uncovered** the true cause or "inner virus" that is creating their cravings or imbalance. As you begin to look at yourself, however, you will find that—layer by layer—issues will be revealed to you that can free you from the past prison of overeating. Doing the exercises outlined in the chapters can actually serve as your master key to release you into a world of freedom where you can say, "I used to have issues with food, but I no longer do. I'm now truly healed."

The Healing Process

Any disorder, imbalance or turmoil you may experience is just a messenger to show you that there is a deeper lesson within, which is **there** to get your attention and show you where you need to grow. When you look at painful inner issues in your life this way, you will be free! **Healing happens from within and is a result of the work you do.** Being cured, on the other hand, comes from external sources and that is not what this process is about. No one can do this work for you; it has to come from within. Rest assured that everything you're asked to do in this book guides you to look within, and will result in real healing.

In order to create anything new, you need to get rid of the old. If you bought new furniture, you would have to remove the old or else there wouldn't be a place for the new furnishings. Your past gunk or inner issues are similar, they're the "old" that need to be recognized and eliminated before the "new" is brought in. The "new" is considered the **result** of healing.

Healing is not fun; it's actually an ugly process even though many people associate the word healing with a pretty picture. They pray for healing, ask for healing, and correlate the idea of healing with a magical concept. Let's take a deeper look, however, into what healing really looks like. You accidentally cut yourself and now there is a huge open wound on your arm. What happens next? First, it bleeds. Then it's stitched up, and then it bruises, swells, and organically grows back together. Next, it's tender and has an ugly discolored scab that eventually falls off and leaves a scar. The scar is pink and delicate, but it's new fresh skin. Finally, over time, the pink scar blends into the original color of the arm, which means that the open wound has healed.

Is that a pretty process? No; it can be painful, stinky, and most unattractive. Along your journey, you may unlock some emotional issues which resemble an open, physical wound. You may even feel that you've discovered an inner wound that has been bleeding for a long, long while. Over time, the issue will stop bleeding, thanks to all the attention you're now giving it, and both you and it will enter the next stage of healing. As you go through the process, you will arrive at the last stage of healing, which is when the sense of freedom emerges.

While you're healing, you might encounter people who say things like, "Wow, seems like you are going through a hard time. Are you okay?" This question is actually an opportunity to be even more okay, because what they may be observing is the bleeding stage. This is your opportunity to ask for support. At this point, you can ask yourself what type of support you need and then clearly communicate that to them. It may sound something like, "Yes, I am going through a hard time. Many issues have been locked inside for quite some time, and I've used food to push them down. My inner gunk needs—and is finally able—to come out. If I don't get in touch with it now, I will continue to use food to push the pain back down. I could use your help. Will you help me? What I really need is encouragement to keep going, and not stop in the middle. I will get there, but I sometimes may need support to just keep going." Remember, healing **is not pretty**! In many cases, things even get a little worse before they ultimately get better. The "worse" is the blood and scabs while the "better" is the final release of the gunk from the past when the scabs fall away, and the end process is true healing. Maybe that's why one of my favorite quotes is: "If you're going through hell, don't stop—keep going—and get to the other side."

Functional Tools for Your Transformation

Now that we understand that food is not the problem, we can begin to see that we have other challenges underneath the surface. So what are these other issues? How do we get in touch with them? And, finally, how do we begin to transform them? This next section is going to answer those questions by giving you effective tools to work with. Once you get familiar with these techniques and know how to apply them, you can then store them in your *Holistic Tool Box* for future use.

Recognize the Internal Alarm

There is an alarm that lives inside each of us. In the past you may have just reacted to this alarm through anger, eating, or fighting with someone, but we actually have the ability to recognize this alarm long before we go into a negative reaction. This alarm can feel like a shift within you where, all of a sudden, you feel like something is off balance and not okay. This alarm, however, is a positive mechanism that we have inside of us to help us stay on track. We just now need to learn to hear it before we subconsciously go into a negative reaction.

The only difference between your alarm and someone else's is **when** you hear it, **how long** it persists and, how you have learned to **shut it off**. At this point, you've probably used food to shut off the alarm. The goal here is to begin to listen and try to find your alarm. What does it sounds like? Can you reflect back and remember the last time it went off? How do you currently deal with the inner noise? Spend a few moments to ask yourself these questions in order to get in touch with your internal alarm. As you begin to hear the alarm, you can then check in with yourself and practice *The Four Questions* (referred to in Chapter 2) to see what set the alarm off. Once you go through this process, you'll begin to create more awareness that will show you when something is seriously off in your life, or when you might just be simply out of balance.

Listen to Your Inner Voice

I once heard my mom refer to prayer as talking to God, while meditation is listening to God. I loved the sound of that because I feel both are important but, the more challenging route is in listening.

Listening to your inner voice is a private and personal "check in" with what is happening within your inner life. Stop, sit down, close your eyes, and go within yourself to find that place of stillness. Begin to ask yourself any question you need an answer to and then **listen**. It is important to not be in chatter mode, but rather to come into your body, out of your head and listen from your heart. The goal here is to find your inner voice, pay attention, and then trust what comes to the surface. A greater "you" is waiting within for the opportunity to speak, but this voice is calm and quiet and you need to get very still in order to hear it. This inner time will create an opening that will help you get to know yourself on a different level, and will also help you begin to engage in the wisdom that already exists inside of you.

Perform an Inner Inventory

Once you are calm, quiet, and still, ask yourself the following questions:

- *How does my body feel?* (**Body**)
- *How am I feeling?* (**Emotions**)
- *What have I been thinking about?* (**Mind**)
- *What have I done to connect to God* (**Spirit**)

This exercise is very open-ended, and the great thing about it is that no one can tell you if you're doing it right or wrong. This is the one place where you are truly the master and can have (and become) all that you are destined to become and achieve.

This simple exercise can either be done on a daily basis or right after the inner alarm has gone off. The goal is to get in touch with your inner environment, develop self awareness, and practice a pause. Here you will learn about yourself on an even deeper level, which will give you information that will eventually unlock your habit of overeating. I encourage you to try this and allow it to take you where it can.

Journal

Write it out and get it out. Don't obsess about the outcome, spelling, grammar, or the way your handwriting looks. Those parts of the process are not important. Your journal is where you can truly be you and get out all the emotional, mental, and spiritual garbage that complicates your life.

As we have discussed in Chapter 1, your body goes to the bathroom because it has a lot of unusable, toxic waste matter left over from the day before, which it no longer needs. Elimination is our body's wise removal system to get rid of what we no longer need and can no longer use.

How do your mind, emotions and spiritual self-perform the same function? This is best accomplished through **journaling**. When you take the time to journal, it's like allowing your mind to excrete waste. Imagine what our bodies would be like if we didn't go to the bathroom. We would die of toxicity. Similarly, what do you think is happening to your "backed-up" mental, emotional and spiritual self? It's toxic with venomous thoughts, and disordered emotions, as well as emptiness and spiritual hunger. Journaling can effectively release all of these inner toxins.

If you are journaling and doing well, I commend you. If you have had some resistance to journaling, I encourage you to give it another try. It's one of the most powerful tools that ended up saving my life! Once you have released some of the waste, you'll create a brand new space for peace.

Become the Inner Listener

Have you ever heard a person say, "You know, I said to myself…" What is going on in that sentence? There are two subjects based in the same person. These two subjects are "I" and "myself". Reminisce for a second, back to a time when you have said that sentence in your mind. Next, ask yourself which subject you are: the "I" or the "myself"? Please take the time to stop for a second and answer that question.

In this sentence, the "I" is the speaker and the "myself" is the listener. I believe that, when we live deep within (where our listener lives), we are the happiest. If, however, we live in the space of the "I", we are probably ruled by our chatter and may even spend time feeling that our truest needs are unheard and unmotivated because there's a constant internal voice that screams at us about our actions. In order for the chatter to have any power, it needs to *speak* to stay alive. The chatter, in essence, is weak, and the second you tell it to stop, it will obey. Once you silence the chatter, it's important to enter the sphere of the listener, and begin to live in this new space.

Pick one of these five functional tools that resonated with you the most, and practice it today. Then, tomorrow, pick another one and practice that for the day. These tools offer guidance (on a step-by-step basis) to get you closer to activating your inner voice. Once the inner voice is activated, you will begin to see that there is an incredible gift available to you, and that all you have to do is **choose to use it**. This gift is **choice**.

You Always Have a Choice

One day I went into a meditation and had a remarkable but simple awareness: **life gives us an incredible gift and it's called "choice"**. Synonyms of choice include "decision", "opportunity", "option", or "preference". This is what life is all about: choice. We can choose to attend or be absent, choose to say yes or no, choose to shout or whisper, choose to be nice or be mean, and so on. These are a few of the many **options** we're given in life, and this is a great thing. Ultimately, you have a choice. **You** decide whether you are going to overeat or stick to a healthy eating plan; **you** decide if you will overindulge or eat a balanced meal. It can, however, feel as if you don't have a choice when your BEMS are out of balance. Right now, perhaps you run to food and overeat because you feel that overeating is your only option. But this is simply not true; you **always** have a choice, and your next assignment will show you how to begin making wise choices everyday!

The Feel Good List

The greatest choice you can make is to decide what you want, over what you don't want. I know that, when I overate, I felt like I didn't have a choice. My cravings would come on so strong that it felt like food turned into oxygen. Over time, I grew so exhausted of feeling sick after I ate that it led me on a search to find out what it was that I **liked**, over what I **disliked**. I began to compile a list with one rule: that I was not able to bite, lick or taste (BLT) the items on my list. I titled the list *Twenty Things That Make Me Feel Good,* and wrote down all sorts of random ideas such as painting my nails (which made me feel like I cared about myself down to my tippy toes), and plucking my eyebrows (which felt like a creative project), and sculpting with clay or watching the wind, etc. **The only goal was to feel good.**

The whole purpose of the list is to point you in a different direction, to give your taste buds a rest, and then give your BEMS an opportunity to show you what really feels good on other levels. This list can then become like a road map to show you different streets to drive down, ones that will take you to a better destination!

You can have anything on your list, but the goal is to list 20 real things that you like or that make you feel good (and are within your reach) in this very moment. They can be simple or complex, passive or active, but no one else can tell **you** what makes **you** feel good except **you**. This assignment becomes a discovery session to get in touch with how you can begin to feel good instead of running to food. Are you ready to feel good? If so, begin creating your list and then practice, practice, practice! Choosing thoughts that feel good will begin to help you disengage from **the continuous appetite** and connect you to your best self.

The Feel Good List

When we overeat, we're giving our body more calories and fat than it needs. As we process through this excess food, it leaves us feeling bad. The goal of this assignment, however, is to begin to feel good. I am certain that there are things in your life that make you feel good right now, but you simply may not be aware of them. This assignment is to help you find 20 things that make you **feel good**, but these need to be the things that you can't BLT – bite, lick, or taste. After you have heard the inner alarm and gotten in touch with what happened within, you'll then have 20 different things to practice, rather than eat.

Please follow these steps to create *The Feel Good List*:

A. *Get out your journal or a separate sheet of paper.*

B. *Think of all the things that make you feel good (regardless of how others might judge it!)*

C. *Next, list up to 20 things that make you feel* **content**, **good**, **happy** *or* **satisfied** *(but no BLT).*

D. *Keep this list visible, refer to it the next time you want to eat, and instead, practice something you've listed.*

If you found this exercise to be helpful,
please store it in your *Holistic Tool Box*

—Chapter 4—
Face Your Overeating

Asking; what, where, when and how will unlock the continuous appetite and lead you into a successful transformation.

I would use food and overeat as my escape. In times of high stress, I'd run to the kitchen as frantically as if I were drowning and needed oxygen. I was behaving like a food addict who needed to overeat in order to release the pain. After I had eaten (and was so over-full that my body would actually get sore), I often wondered, *"What am I trying to push down with food? What is it that hurts SO much? What am I trying to escape? Is it a feeling, a person, a situation, or maybe even a thought? What's inside me that I find frightening?"* As I persistently overate, these questions continued to surface. Over time, I grew so sick of repeating the same questions that I finally sat down and decided to answer them. Little did I know that I was about to unlock a major awareness that would ultimately set me free from my abusive relationship with food and overeating.

As I sat down to write, I realized that the main issue I had to confront was the challenge of dealing with the ordinary things in life. I had negative feelings and thoughts toward most situations, and would sabotage both my body and my spirit because of my inability to effectively handle these circumstances. At that very moment, I understood my problem: **I didn't know how to deal with what was happening in my life, so I continuously overate to distract myself from what was occurring.**

When we don't know how to face ourselves or the life issues that confront us, we often try to escape the situation rather than deal with what is going on. These escape patterns are simply a learned technique to **avoid** the issue presented (mostly because we've never been **taught** how to actually **deal** with the issue on hand). There isn't a life-skill's class in high school that teaches you how to have a healthy relationship, find your own purpose, interview successfully, effectively manage your money, or even organize your life and time. We aren't taught these essential skills, which means we are often dumbfounded when we find ourselves in an ordinary situation which requires us to respond with a specific skill that we don't have. Therefore, we learn to **escape.**

If you struggle with your weight, you've learned to use **food** as your form of escape. Food then distracts you (or your BEMS) from what you're truly experiencing. This pattern, however, will invariably trap you because food will only provide relief for a moment or two and then, the second you stop chewing, you'll be right back where you started: confused and out of touch. And to complicate matters, you'll be so full and focused on the food you've eaten that you can't even think about the situation you were running from in the first place. The bottom line is that there has to be a better way to give yourself some much-needed relief from what seems to be so overwhelming. That better way is through **facing yourself.**

How To Face Yourself

When you begin to recognize that something is wrong within, rather than outside of you, you'll begin to transform the escape pattern provided by food. I had a client who told me, "You know, I am good with my eating regimen when it comes to breakfast and lunch, but then, when it's dinner time, I eat way too much. I munch before dinner and then I snack on sweets afterwards! What is happening and why can't I control myself at night?" My first question to her was, "What's happening at night that you don't want to face?" She paused and then replied, "I have trouble winding down. I love booting up in the morning and getting things done. After everything is done, however, I don't know what to do with myself, so I eat." She paused and then understood. "OH! I'm trying to escape from not knowing what to do with myself at night, the only time of the day when there is nothing left to do!"

We then discussed her anxiety of **not knowing what to do with herself**. She felt so much relief from acknowledging it that we then came up with a list of many different activities she could try **in place of eating**. As she began to practice things like playing family board games, sewing, swinging in her hammock, and many other uncomplicated activities, she found a sense of enjoyment at the end of her day. And, not surprisingly, her after-hours **continuous appetite** subsided.

It doesn't always have to be some HUGE issue that's lurking in the shadows. It can be as simple as not knowing what to do with yourself or as complicated as the inability to navigate your way through a troublesome relationship. That's why it's so important to come face-to-face with the issue inside and see what is happening in there. Once you've identified the inner problem, you can make a different choice and begin to get in touch with how and what it is that you try to escape from. Think back to the last time you overate to gain insight on how you can face yourself instead of escape, and then ask yourself the five *Escape Pattern Questions:*

1. *What was happening when I chose to overeat?*
2. *What did I do to handle the situation?*
3. *What emotion did the circumstances make me feel?*
4. *What other things can I do when I feel that same emotion?*
5. *When I find myself in this situation again, what can my future-self do instead of eat?*

After you take the time to answer these questions you may find that there are many things going on within you that may seem scary on the surface but, when you face them, they will weaken. When we escape, it just takes us farther and farther away from what we want. These questions, however, will help you identify what makes you escape, and what you can do instead of escaping which is to face yourself.

How to Face the Body's Weight Loss Trap

Susan walks in with a bewildered look on her face and then says, (in an irritated tone), "I just want to lose ten pounds. Everything in my life would be better if I could lose these ten pounds but, for some reason, I just can't lose this annoying weight." Are you, like Susan, constantly struggling with your weight? Do you have thoughts like: *"If I could just lose this (#) pounds, my life would be better."*? **If so, this is simply an escape from dealing with your real issues disguised as a quest for weight loss.**

When I lost seventy-five pounds, I assumed that my life would be different and better. Don't get me wrong; some things did change, like my pant and bra size, and even the looks I received on the street. But, in the grand scheme of things, once you arrive at the new weight, these things mean so little. The things that I thought would change—that I subconsciously wanted to change—**did not** change. For instance, I thought that, if I could just see a specific number on the scale, I would feel good about (and proud of) myself. But the truth was that I used "weight loss" as a tool to convince myself that "one day," my body would finally be good enough.

This tool of "convincing" and the idea of "one day" were escape mechanisms to help me avoid facing the truth: that I hated myself as well as my body. I had convinced myself that weight loss would allow me to accept myself, which is like a guy thinking, *"If I get a BMW, I won't ever be lonely again on a Saturday night."* **Wrong**! Weight loss has nothing to do with **acceptance**, just as a BMW has nothing to do with loneliness. No weight loss, aesthetic surgery, or pharmaceutical drug can help you love, accept or be in harmony with yourself. My basic problem was self-hatred and once I recognized the real issue and began to love my body—in that exact moment, just the way it was, I began to build a better relationship with myself.

Don't get me wrong, there is nothing wrong with wanting to lose weight, as long as it's for the right reasons. Some of the right reasons might include assisting your body to be at its best, experiencing wellness, feeling fit, moving with more ease, playing with your kids, or traveling more freely. When you get the inner issues out of the way and see what weight loss can truly give you, you get on the right track for healthy weight loss. This requires a commitment to honor your body, fuel it appropriately, and remember to befriend it along the way!

As I spoke to Susan about her struggle with her "last ten pounds", I asked her what she thought "weight loss" would bring to her life. Her answer was fascinating: "I need to have more organization and structure in my life and, when I follow a strict eating plan, my life feels balanced. But, when I have an extra ten pounds on me, I feel out of control." Susan clearly painted a picture that said she needed organization and structure in her life, but the only way she had ever experienced the organization or structure she needed in the past was by a restricted eating regimen.

Next, we spoke about how Susan could organize her life around something **other than food**. We spoke about running her day differently, setting up a schedule, and then even prioritizing interruptions with an importance scale. Later that year, Susan came to me and admitted, "I never realized how I'd structured my life around food. By applying this simple change of structure, I've experienced freedom in both my life and my relationship with food."

So many people fall into the trap of thinking that, if their body were skinnier, life would be better. Simply stated: **weight loss makes you smaller, not more significant; it makes you lighter, not more lovable; it makes you thinner, not more thrilling.** The truth is that weight loss brings weight loss and, if you get too caught up in the idea of losing weight, it can be just a way to try to escape from yourself. Now it's time to answer this question for yourself: **what do you think weight loss will bring you?**

After you look within, answer that question and discover that you may truly want other things in life (like a different job, to be a better person, make a positive difference in the world, or just be kinder to other people), you can begin to work toward those things—which have absolutely nothing to do with losing fat. This practice then frees you to start a healthy eating plan for the right reasons.

How to Face the Emotional Excuse

First we have **thought**, then we have **feelings**, and those feelings are what inspire **action**. Emotions are a light form of energy with a powerful effect. When our excuses are left undiagnosed, however, they invariably turn into emotional ignorance, which detrimentally fuels **the continuous appetite**. And, once the appetite is triggered, we eat and eat and eat until we end up in a disempowered state.

Have you ever found yourself in an emotional state that sounds like this: "*I ate too much and feel powerless over my cravings. I hate this struggle with food!*"? This is just an emotional excuse that has nothing to do with the real problem. The real problem was the emotions that were waiting to be acknowledged and released but had instead been ignored and pushed down with food.

To transform these emotional excuses—**the feelings of being powerless over food**—it is important to first accept that these are just excuses, and are **not** the truth. The truth is that you have power within you, but it is being used in a way that hurts rather than helps. At this point, your emotions may be under-acknowledged, which can yield the end result of an overeating episode. Overeating (a toxic behavior) has become the way you get your own attention, and it's a survival technique which you've applied to try and reach an inner homeostasis. But, since food only ends up making matters worse, we need to **find a different way to allow our emotions to have a balanced voice**. That way is through an inventory of what you emotionally feel within.

We have two main emotions: **Love** and **Fear**. Simply said, everything that feels **good** comes from **love**, everything that feels **bad** comes from **fear**. Let's take a look at some of the emotions that come from **love** and feel **good**:

accepted	faithful	relaxed
adored	grateful	romantic
balanced	gratified	safe
calm	happy	satisfied
caring or cared for	harmonious	secure
cheerful	healthy	self-acceptance
comforted	helpful	self-acknowledgement
complete	joyful	self-approval
composed	loved or loving	self-assured
content	nurtured or nurturing	self-fulfilled
delighted	peaceful	self-reliance
enthusiastic	pleased	serene
excited	protected	trusted or trusting

This is just a fraction of the emotions that we are able to release, but I'm sure you get the idea. If you can begin to accurately identify what you are feeling, you will gain power over continuous eating.

How many of these **good** feelings are you in touch with on a daily basis? Do you want to see a brighter light in your life? Begin to ask yourself what you feel in the moment and then be willing to come out of your comfort zone.

Next, let's look at some of the emotions that come from **fear** and feel **bad:**

abandoned	frustrated	resentful
aggravated	furious	restless
angry	hesitant	sad
annoyed	hurt	self-hatred
anxious	indifferent	self-sabotage
bitter	insecure	self-judged
conflicted	insignificant	skeptical
cynical	jealous	tense

depressed	lonely	threatened
disgusted	needy	unappreciated
doubtful	neglectful	unsure
envious	offended	upset
fearful	rejected	worried

Do any of these emotions seem familiar? Are you more in touch with the bad feelings than the good ones? If so, this may be one of your serious emotional imbalances. It's so important to feel good in this life (the word good is similar to the word God, with just one extra O). If you constantly feel bad, then that's a sign that it is time for a change. Face your emotions and begin asking yourself what you are truly feeling and which emotion is surfacing. And remember, every step you have walked along your journey up to this point has been in its perfect place. So exhale and—with eyes wide open—begin to look at your emotions and feelings as they surface.

Face the Mental Ambush

Our outlook and attitude is directly linked to (and comes from) our mentality. Negative and repetitive mentality can frequently create thinking patterns that end up getting in our way. When this happens, we often tend to ask questions that actually create breakdowns instead of breakthroughs.

One way we escape mentally is through a miniature word in our language—one that many people employ frequently—and that word is "why"? Why questions only lead you to ask yet another "why". This is the philosophical cycle that spins you around and around. Instead of leading you to any answers, it just stirs up more why questions.

For example: *Why do I have to struggle with food?* Because the immediate escape you found happened to be food, and it became your drug of choice. *Why?* Because that's what you discovered along the way, and it helped you escape from whatever your painful thoughts were. *Why?* Because that is what food does. It distracts you from focusing on what's really going on. *Why?* The person who asks "why" can always follow the answer with another unsatisfied "why", but this process typically leaves you mentally displeased, unfulfilled, and exhausted.

As a situation falls into your lap, begin to ask different questions and you'll arrive at more insightful answers. I encourage you to practice inserting new questions into your inner dialogue because this new application will help you observe different answers. Begin to ask **what, when, where** and **how** questions.

- **What** is your struggle with food about? *I struggle with food because I have outrageous cravings that I have to act on, which turn my brain off and take me into different thoughts.*
- **When** do you struggle with food? *I struggle mostly at night and on the weekends.*
- **Where** do you struggle with food the most? *I struggle with food at events, at the grocery store, at my in-laws' and parents' houses, on most weeknights, when I'm drinking alcohol, and on the weekends.*
- **How** do you struggle with food during those times? *It seems to be the "once I pop I can't stop" mentality. I do okay if I don't*

> *go off my eating plan but, the second I diverge from that plan,*
> *it all goes downhill.*

These questions begin to scratch the surface of what's really going on, and they can take you on an insightful and progressive path. Once you have some answers, you can re-word the questions that most closely apply to you in your current situation. This process will walk you deeper and deeper down the rabbit hole of self-awareness. The next layer of questions would be:

- **What** does eating more food do for you?
- **When** do you find that the "once you pop you can't stop" mentality kicks in the most?
- **Where** do you do this eating, and who is around?
- **How** can you begin to get in touch with what you really want?

Rather than continuing to escape, use the what, when, where and how questions to check in mentally and *face your mind and thinking patterns.*

How to Face the Spiritual Wake-up Call

I love the concept that we are spiritual beings having human experiences. When I speak about spirit, I'm referring to a force within you that goes beyond your body. Plainly said, it's the essence that makes YOU inside your body. It's the core that is connected to God, love, and life. In reference to "waking up", we all have this experience available to us, and it's called a **spiritual awakening**.

Have you ever been sitting down, crossed-legged, and then have your foot fall asleep? As it wakes up, you might have the awareness, *"Wow, my foot is tingling and I can't remember the last time I even thought about my foot."* Then, it begins to tingle more, which is slightly uncomfortable, but the tingles represent blood flow, which is the foot's way of coming back to consciousness.

This is an example of what a spiritual wake-up call can feel like. All of a sudden, you're awake without even realizing that you had been asleep. You then get a little uncomfortable, because your spirit is requiring more energy and effort to keep it awake. Once that stage is over, you are fully conscious and thankful for a functioning spirit.

Being awake is like getting a new pair of glasses and seeing things clearly for the first time, when before, you didn't even realize that life was out of focus. You can invite this process into your life through prayer or meditation but what's most important is to **have the desire to wake up**. That is when you will discover a whole new way of being alive. The awakening will happen to you through this journey when you reach the point where you're ready for it and you allow it. I encourage you to continue to invite God into your life on a daily basis. Being awake is an act of:

- choosing to connect with God
- living in the present moment
- facing your reality
- choosing your next step mindfully

When we choose to reach out to God rather than eat, we are taking a powerful step toward transformation.

Healing will happen as you practice all these techniques. Through the application, you will begin to move further and further away from continuous overeating and into a place where you really get to know and love yourself. I promise you that, above all other voices, the most profound answers are those that come from within, and my intention is to help you finally get in touch with that inner voice. Asking **what**, **where**, **when** and **how** will unlock **the continuous appetite** and lead you into a successful transformation.

—Inner-Query Four—

The Positive Response

This exercise is based on creating a productive way to deal with what is in front of you. Please follow this process whenever you find yourself in a difficult life situation.

A. *First, stop and look at how you reacted to a person and/ or a situation in your life.*

B. *Next, acknowledge the feelings and thoughts that surfaced inside you.*

C. *Then, answer the questions bellow to create your new Positive Response:*

1. *How do I feel?*
2. *What do I want now?*
3. *Can I get what I want from where I am right now?*
4. *If not, where do I need to go?*

If you found this exercise to be helpful,
please store it in your *Holistic Tool Box.*

—Chapter 5—
Diets Cause Cravings

As you tune in to your negative thoughts about food, your attention will shift away from the continuous appetite and you'll be directed toward the awareness of what you actually want.

Have you ever heard someone say, "I can't go there, or do that because, I am on a diet?" This behavior is usually a sign that the person is controlled by "diet thinking". While there are many "diets" that are healthy and help people achieve goals, there are also consequences that come from dieting. These unhealthy and over-restrictive patterns can actually awaken and stimulate **the continuous appetite**.

Diet thinking is the mental fuel that ultimately restricts you because of all the limits it puts on your behavior. Diets eventually leave you **feeling** like "you can't have this", which turns into a vicious cycle and feels bad. Then food acts as a weapon to try to destroy whatever it is that feels bad. Whenever you spend a large amount of time thinking about your food intake, with the goal of losing weight, you put yourself in a limited pattern that continues to see "blocks" and **what you are not allowed to eat**. I am not saying that all diets are bad. Instead, I just want to point out that when there are destructive issues underneath your weight-loss desires, you'll need to work through those issues first in order to successfully lose the weight, and keep it off.

Do you have the tendency to get stuck in "diet thinking"? If so, can you see how all those restrictions actually act as a massive catalyst to send you into the kitchen? Rather than continuing to restrict yourself with diet thinking, try instead to use all that energy to look into what is really going on **behind** both the craving and the desire to lose weight.

Just One More Bite

Do you ever say to yourself; *"Just one more bite (or another serving, or another taste) and then I'll be satisfied!"?* If so, you might be familiar with the many reasons and endless excuses upon why you need *"just one more bite"*. In the meantime, the action of *"one more bite"* has the potential to become repetitive and addictive, which turns into a food splurge that leaves you feeling worse than you did before. Why is this? Why doesn't the craving go away after that infamous "bite"? Because the craving is not for food in that moment. It's disguised as food, but it's truly just your inner self crying out in a desperate bid to get your own attention.

When I was about to indulge in a craving, it felt as if I would go from zero to a hundred in one second flat. I was so overpowered by the *intensity* of the craving that my thoughts seemed to push the food right into my mouth before I was even aware of what was happening. I'd immediately begin to eat, eat, eat, and feel a brief sense of comfort and satisfaction. But then that sense of comfort would fade—fast. As the brief good feeling faded, I found my mouth wrapped around even more food—again trying to chase the feeling of comfort—but the food only touched it for an instant. I needed, therefore, "just one more bite" to regain that short-lived sense of satisfaction.

Cravings are your reminder to recognize that food is simply the messenger and not the problem. The problem, however, is that you need the comfort of your own attention and it's time to give it to yourself. To find the message that hides underneath your cravings, please grab your journal and answer the following questions:

- *What made me want to eat?*
- *What motivated me to think food would make it better?*
- *What might have triggered me earlier in the day?*

The answers to these questions will help you begin to get a glimpse into what is happening in your BEMS, and what the messages underneath the cravings are all about.

The War Against Yourself

You've probably begun to notice that eating doesn't make you feel better, improve your circumstances, or even help you escape anymore. This is because you've now had an awareness, an insight that the issue is within yourself, rather than with the food. Awareness is like a stretch mark in the mind; once it's expanded, it will not go back to its former size. This is why eating and food may have lost all previously effective power to help you feel better.

At this point, when you overeat, binge or mindlessly shove food into your mouth, food is simply being used as ammunition to continue **the war against** yourself. This "war" persistently shoots down whatever "willpower" you have left, and leaves you feeling defeated. The war goes like this: first, the enemy appears (the craving), then the weapon (overeating) is activated. This creates the war, or feeling of defeat.

This war has developed over time from a habitual pattern of thinking negative **thoughts,** which created horrible **feelings,** and turned into self-defeating **actions**, bringing us full-circle to more cravings. This cycle viciously repeats itself until you're ready and willing to break the inner rotation of negative thoughts, bad feelings, and disempowering actions.

Are you ready to end the war against yourself and your cravings? The process of setting yourself free is a simple three-part equation that will give you a better understanding of what is happening. The three-part process goes as follows: Part A is your **thought**, Part B is the **feeling** it activates, and Part C is the **action** it creates. Therefore, when you think thoughts, and feel feelings, you'll continuously create actions.

Part A: The Thought

When the thought is negative or feels bad, the feeling and action will follow and be negative or feel bad as well. For example you might think, *"I just need to lose weight and get my body back into shape. Then everything in my life will be better. But something always seems to come up, and I find myself on vacation getting donuts for the family, and all my weight loss goals get thrown out the window."* This is Part A of the equation, the **thought**, or the negative mentality of the war that creates a feeling.

Part B: The Feeling

Part B is that you then release a sequential **feeling** that you may or may not be aware of: *"I hate my life and myself. I feel so **bad** about how I look and feel, and this little donut gives me at least one moment of gratification."* This bad **feeling** is actually the motivation that continues to fuel your food choices and is what triggers Part C, the **action.** Then, once at the donut shop (subconsciously **thinking** and consequently **feeling** bad about yourself and life), you choose to take **action** on your craving.

Part C: The Action

Part C is the act of boycotting your goals by eating a couple of donuts. That's why thinking that Part C is the problem leaves you with no equation to fix the dilemma. If you look back, however, and see that, in order to change Part C, you need to closely examine Part A and B, you will empower yourself. Beginning to follow a different formula will lead you to a better place.

Change Your Thoughts, Change Your Actions

Our minds have tremendous influence over and impact upon our feelings and actions. That's why if the mind is powerful in a negative direction, it can be equally powerful in a positive direction—toward what you **do** want. The best place to start is on Part A, which is the recognition of your thoughts, and then the other parts will click together simultaneously! Apply this process by asking yourself what **thoughts** you think, then look at how those thoughts make you **feel**, and what **action** they ultimately inspire.

Next, remember to first see the craving as a messenger that is delivering information about the thoughts you have been thinking. At this point, I encourage you to try to refrain from eating, and instead ask yourself *The Four Questions* from Chapter 2. Finally, use the information you find, and begin transforming and replacing those negative thoughts with **what you DO want.** Applying this process will transform the former negative rotation of thoughts, feelings, and actions into a positive awareness over your BEMS!

Healing Your Body's Eating Habits

We all have to eat to stay alive, and there's simply no way around that fact. It's important, however, to honestly know your own body's eating habits and what you do with food on a daily basis—all excuses aside. I encourage you to write down everything you eat or BLT (bite, lick or taste) for three whole days. Tracking your food intake will help you become more honest about what is actually going into your mouth and why the scale reflects the number it does.

There are so many suggestions about how to eat healthy foods, what not to eat, what time to eat, what foods to mix together, etc.. When I began my own research, I came across so many different programs and now, ten years later, I have a blended approach that works well for me. I eat every three hours, start my day with thirty grams of protein (a suggestion from Tim Ferriss, author of THE FOUR HOUR BODY), eat "brunch" every day because I love the idea of brunch, eat both a banana and apple for snacks and, for dinner, typically eat chicken breasts, a green vegetable and a legume, and always end the meal with a serving of dark chocolate. Please recognize that finding your eating plan and flow with food takes time, trial and error. I did not come up with my food plan overnight; it took me years to find what was best for me.

I encourage you, however, to practice whatever approach to food you know works for you. If you don't currently have a healthy eating plan, please stop and research several different healthy eating philosophies, choose the plan you like best—one that is moderate, healthy, and works within your lifestyle—and then incorporate that program into your daily life. I follow a more strict approach Sunday through Thursday and then allow more pleasure on Friday and Saturday. If any of these suggestions sound good to you, please give them a try. If these suggestions sound unreasonable, just let them go and seek out what echoes a synergistic feeling to you.

I encourage you to apply the same intention with the following suggestions. These are easy-to-use eating tips that you can incorporate into your everyday food schedule. The goal of these techniques is to get you physically ready to embrace a new healthier relationship with food.

Eat a Serving of Food Every Three Hours

Think of a guy who works in a busy office. If he is handed a pile of work and is able to get through the work before the next pile arrives, he will not have the original pile still sitting on his desk. Why? Because it has already been processed and completed. Therefore, take the size of your palm and consider that your "pile of work". Then, every three hours, put that size of food into your body and you'll be able to process it without storing it as fat. When you eat an appropriate amount of food every three hours, your stomach is able to digest it, turn it into energy, and then burn off the rest. When we place too much food in our stomach (overeat), we cannot burn it all so it then gets stored as fat. Larger portion sizes of food are like huge piles of unfinished work that are sitting on our desk, creating a mess. If you eat small portions every three hours, you will be assisting your body's metabolism to burn, process, and turn your food into usable positive energy.

Eat Half, Leave Half

We all have lives that require us to visit—at one time or another— restaurants and eat meals. As we know, most restaurant portions are about triple the size of a healthy portion. Restaurants also cook with excessive amounts of butter, fat, oil, and sugar. Therefore, a great rule to apply is *Eat Half, Leave Half.* You might have heard this suggestion before but, if you truly apply it, it works! Here's what you can do: when you get your plate, ask for a take-out box, cut your portions in half and place half in the box. Eat the other half (the one that is in front of you), be present as you eat, and truly enjoy the food. Then, in at least three hours, if you get hungry, you can eat the rest. When you *eat half and leave half,* you give both your body and your stomach the appropriate amount of food (and the necessary time) to be able to digest what you've eaten and turn the meal into energizing fuel.

Find Your Power Food

Your power food is whatever you eat that is natural and specifically makes **you** feel clean, fueled and healthy. Do you know what your personal power food is? Does anything come to mind? If so, then this is the food that you have synergy with that breaks down and produces clean fuel in your body.

In order to find this food, it's important to get all the artificial and processed foods out of your body so you are starting with a clean palate. Once you have this fresh place within, ask yourself what food makes you feel good, strong and clean. Sit with this question for a while. If nothing comes to mind, research a list of alkaline foods such as avocado, apple cider vinegar, broccoli, celery, grapes, kelp, lemon, mango, papaya, parsley, watercress, and watermelon. Read through the list and pay attention to how you feel when reading them. If a specific food stands out, pay attention because it just may be your power food. Next, try eating the food and see how it makes you feel. If you feel great, begin incorporating that food into your daily eating regimen.

Only Eat TWO Junk Foods Per Week

We all have taste buds, and they're in our mouth to remind us to eat. The role of these little sensory protrusions, however, is not to dictate our palate's relationship with food; instead it's to assist in fueling the body. Junk foods are items that have very low nutritional value, but make taste buds sing. In your weekly eating regimen, there is room for only **one serving** of two of these foods every seven days.

Do you know which two junk foods you really love and could simply never give up? Ask yourself this question, and see what immediately comes to mind. Try to notice what it is that you **love** about the food. Is it the creaminess? Crunchiness? Saltiness or sweetness? The answer will help you get in deeper touch with what this food specifically does for you. Next, narrow it down to two foods, and allow yourself to have **one serving** of each food per week. If, however, you find that you love a whole meal, please limit that indulgence to one time per month.

The "junk foods" that I have found most people can relate to are:

burgers	cookies
brownies	donuts
burritos	french fries
cake	ice cream
candy bars	mac n' cheese
cheese fries	pizza
chocolate	potato chips
Coca-Cola	soda

These foods may taste exceptional, but they will wreak havoc on your waistline if eaten on a daily basis. Therefore, you want to know what you love, narrow it down to two foods, allow yourself one serving of each food per week and, when you eat the food, enjoy every bite! Below are some ways that you can creatively enjoy your favorite foods:

- When you eat a **burger**, go for the real thing but take the other half home.
- Eat one **brownie** bite, and learn to just have one.
- When you order a **burrito**, ask if they have whole-wheat tortillas and order a light portion of cheese.
- Eat one small **cupcake** instead of a big wedge of cake.
- Make room in your calories to afford ONE **dark chocolate candy bar**.
- Take one ounce of your **cheese fries** on a small plate, and only eat those.

- When you want **chocolate**, eat dark chocolate chips, 32 chips is one serving.
- Go ahead and eat ONE **cookie**, but choose your favorite and enjoy it.
- For a **donut**, try a donut-hole instead and chew it twenty times.
- Order **fries**, but only pick up a light handful with your fingers and don't let the fries touch your palm. Then, place them on a separate plate and only eat one ounce (or that portion).
- Order a small **ice-cream**.
- Make homemade **mac n' cheese** using whole wheat pasta, and substitute cottage cheese instead of full-fat cheese.
- Order a flat bread **pizza** with veggies and chicken.
- Weigh one ounce of **potato chips**, place in a bowl, and put the rest away.
- Have a real can of **Coca-Cola**, but limit it to only once per week.

Once you narrow down your two favorite foods and then allow yourself to have one serving of both these foods per week, you will be inviting a pleasant enjoyment into your life! Next, stop and notice how you feel when you're with these foods. When I finally figured out what my taste buds truly wanted, not craved, I was actually able to experience satisfaction from food. After you find your two favorite junk foods, research them to learn what the actual serving size is, and then practice eating that exact amount. Finally, allow yourself to truly enjoy one serving of each fare—per week.

Practice Healthy Eating Etiquette

It's important to have good manners, and it's so easy to throw that smart eating behavior out the window when life gets busy and hectic. The simplicity of these manners, however, can truly help you slow down and gain awareness of your relationship with food. From this point forward, make the commitment to only eat:

- in a calm environment
- in a seated position
- using a plate to put your food on and a fork to feed yourself
- chewing each bite of your food twenty times, with your mouth closed
- while taking a deep breath in between bites

When you practice this eating etiquette, you will probably see your feelings of worthiness increase. Once this happens, you will begin to change on a deep inner level and you'll set yourself free from past negative behavior.

When these positive feelings are activated, you will be winding down the war on yourself as well as decreasing the use of restrictive diets, which only make cravings worse. Remember, cravings are simply your reminder to recognize that food is only the messenger that is trying to get your attention to look within and heal the true problem. As you tune into your negative thoughts about food, your attention will shift away from **the continuous appetite** and direct you toward the awareness of what you actually want.

—Inner-Query Five—

The Message Beneath the Craving

This exercise helps you get in touch with the difference between being hungry and having a craving. Hunger is a physiological need, while a craving typically originates from a deep inner emotional, mental or spiritual need. Please ask yourself these four simple questions to find *The Message Beneath the Craving*:

1. *Did I eat enough today?*
2. *What am I truly hungry for?*
3. *What is really going on in this moment?*
4. *How can I get what I need?*

If you found this exercise to be helpful,
please store it in your *Holistic Tool Box*.

—Chapter 6—
How the Heck Do I Only Eat Half?

To slim the continuous appetite, find the hole that food is trying to fill and give yourself what you actually desire.

E at half and then leave half? Yeah, right! When I first heard this concept it seemed as if it had come from another planet. How the heck do I only eat half? Half of a burger? One donut hole? A piece of pizza? Are you *crazy*?! Many others have asked that same question so, if this idea seems like a hard pill to swallow, I understand.

When I used to binge-eat, it seemed like a dis-empowering voice was saying, *"Who cares, stop counting, keep eating, eat everything,"* which is the complete opposite of *eating half and leaving half.* Whenever I listened to that disempowering voice, I'd overeat and then wake up the following morning with a horrible feeling that I had cheated on myself. I was way too familiar with this feeling because it happened on a weekly basis which, in turn, made it next to impossible for me to feel happy with my life, myself and my body.

This disempowering voice can say many things to encourage you to eat, such as, *"Have another serving, because more will taste even better,"* or, *"you don't want to stop now, it tastes too good,"* or, *"forget eating half, eat it ALL!"* These statements, however, are false because more **won't** taste better and you **can** learn to just have a little.

The truth—when it comes to eating—is that nothing tastes better than the first couple of bites. The first couple of bites are flavorful, aromatic, and new but, after about three bites, the tasteful experience is over. The food in front of you, at that moment, has essentially lost its flavorful power to excite you. This doesn't mean we only eat a couple of bites of all food, because it may take more than that to actually fuel up. This one-half technique is primarily for junk foods and eating out.

Americans have the unfortunate (and unhealthy) habit of using food for so many reasons that have absolutely nothing to do with food, including to celebrate, communicate, entertain and socialize. We are actually missing the point of—and have lost touch with—what food is for. I'm not saying go the opposite extreme and **only** use food for fuel. But what I am advocating is to be balanced and practice moderation when it comes to eating. Our past habits with food have created the blueprint for how we presently use food to experience excitement, flavor and satisfaction, which is why it can be so hard to just eat half. There is a great deal of emotional expectation riding on that next bite. Feelings of excitement, pleasure, satisfaction, and stimulation seem to be the promises that rest inside every spoonful, but *this is not food's purpose.* We find ourselves, therefore, using the same flawed excuse in order to eat more, the excuse that just one more bite will give us a quick look at fulfillment.

There are a couple of things going on here. First, you may want more contentment, enjoyment, and fulfillment in your life and, if this emotional need has been left unacknowledged, you've begun to use food to help yourself touch those feelings. This is like needing a massage and making an appointment with your cell phone provider. The two have nothing to do with each other and, therefore, cannot give you what you truly need. This lack of acknowledgement toward what it is you truly need is the reason why another bite seems so intriguing. There is no doubt about it, you DO have a need for "something", but that need has very little (if anything) to do with food and taking another bite.

Please begin to ask yourself, a) what is missing from your life and, b) how you can give that to yourself. Once you begin this investigation, you'll stop eating for the wrong reasons, which will help you learn how to eat the appropriate amount of food. The reason it may have seemed difficult in the past for you to *eat half and leave half* is because you probably used food to experience excitement, fun, the flavor of life, and satisfaction. Thankfully, now you're finally ready to meet the real thing—instead of a taste-bud substitute.

Uncovering the LIES!

If you find yourself thinking, *"This is so good. I want more. Give me more,"* your chatter is actually creating a false idea that more will taste **even better** and will **actually satisfy you.** This chatter will then also tell you, *"It's too hard to eat only half and leave the other half."* Recognize that these are **lies** and learn to silence them. The truth is, you truly only experience and enjoy those first few bites and eating more is simply chasing a lie.

So the better question becomes, *"How do I overcome all these lies?"* The answer is simple. Lies are chatter, which is transient thought energy and just happens to be the easiest, lightest, and quickest form of energy to change. So silence this chatter and recognize that this misleading mentality will sneak up on you from time to time, but it is (and will always be) a LIE. Next, disengage from the lie by looking for the truth.

The truth—unlike chatter—is rock solid and, because of that, you will always be able to make a connection by looking within. When I began to look within, I found that I had used food to fill up the empty holes inside of me. I had holes from feeling unloved, rejected, and even feeling that I didn't deserve to be happy. Those holes were deep within, and it took me a long time to unearth them. Previously, they had spoken to me through chocolate cravings but, once I located the source of the pain, the cravings simply evaporated.

I got in touch with my pain through journaling, meditating, reading books, seeking spiritual healing, and talking it out with my ever-attentive and understanding mom. This all led me to begin to effectively see what I was ultimately longing for, which was love and acceptance. I then had the awareness that I was the only one who could give that to myself. I realized that what occurred in the past had happened to teach me some powerful lessons, and it was now time to **give myself** all that I felt had been withheld from me in the past. And those inner blessings—like love and acceptance—had nothing to do with chocolate.

We all have holes inside of us, but this emptiness has nothing to do with food. Instead, it has to do with unfulfilling past life situations. The holes of the past, however, are really tools that can help to heal the broken and hurtful parts of you. The things that have been broken are now ready to be repaired and **rebuilt even stronger**! Therefore, if you know that you have these inner holes, you can now locate them, heal them, and begin to eliminate the misguided use of food to fill them up.

<u>Stop Filling Those Holes with Food</u>

As mentioned before, these first few bites don't have any more or less "flavor" than the rest, but they're what your taste buds enthusiastically recognize and welcome. We continue eating and blindly chase this initial experience, which felt good, because we think that continued eating will maintain that same feeling. The act of eating at this point, however, is a counter-productive indulgence that is much more about biting, chewing and filling up rather than tasting.

There are many healthy ways to fill your inner holes and, now that we know we've been trying to fill them with food, we can make a different choice. The first step is to know what foods you truly love (Chapter 5), and narrow that list down to two. It's important to understand that it's okay if the foods you love happen to be junk food. The tricky part, however, is to learn how to just eat an appropriate amount. To take the process a step further, notice what happens when you are with your favorite foods and take the time to ask yourself the *Food Inquiry Questions* as you eat that specific food.

- *What do I think food will give me?*
- *What memories are triggered?*
- *What thoughts come to mind?*
- *What am I feeling?*
- *What do I truly desire?*

The answers to these questions will help you unlock some of the needs you may have, and gain awareness of the inner issues that you are now ready to work through and heal. If, however, you find yourself saying that the answer is a need and desire for more food, go deeper and ask, "How do I think more food will serve me in this moment?" When you land upon a concrete answer, give yourself whatever it is you ultimately want. The bottom line is that we all have a hole within us and we can now figure out what we want, give that to ourselves, and—ultimately—stop trying to fill up the holes with food.

At this moment, my hope is that you're beginning to recognize that the first few bites of food are all you accurately taste and truly enjoy. This concept may take some personal analysis to really "get", but I encourage you to trust the fact that food and eating will never solve the current discomfort in your life. We need food to fuel our bodies, which is why it is important to make nourishing, healthy choices. On the other hand, it's okay to occasionally indulge and satisfy your taste-buds with treats as well. Once you see this duality as truth, you'll begin to dissolve **the continuous appetite**.

<u>Positively Filling the Holes in Your Life</u>

Do you want abundance, comfort, direction, ease, energy, excitement, free time, fulfillment, fun, love, motivation, reassurance, relaxation, and romance? Well, these feelings or experiences have little to do with food and eating. Up to this point, however, you may have used burgers, brownies, burritos, cake, candy bars, cheese fries, chocolate, cookies, donuts, french fries, ice-cream, mac n' cheese, pizza, potato chips, and soda to try to activate some of these powerful feelings. But food, however, cannot manifest these feelings. If you want to experience the feelings mentioned above, a more productive approach would be to try the following:

- For more **abundance**: Begin to practice self-acceptance, particularly for where you are at this moment. This act will fill you up internally and might unlock some emotional gunk that is ready to be released.

- For more **comfort**: Give yourself a hug by wrapping your arms around your chest, close your eyes, and say to yourself sincerely, *"I love you."*

- For **direction** in life: Begin to connect with God by practicing some of the earlier tips mentioned (Chapter 4) and genuinely ask—from your heart—for the next step.

- For more **ease**: Take a deep breath, and ask yourself if you will even remember this in a year. If not, learn to release the negativity.

- For more **energy**: Get enough sleep, think in positive terms, and reduce your daily caffeine intake.

- For more **excitement**: Find two things that excite you, and then try to creatively experience them on a weekly basis.

- For more **free time**: Look over how you are currently spending your time, and immediately begin to schedule an hour each day just for yourself.

- For more **fulfillment**: Ask yourself what you love to do, and then work on incorporating that activity into your daily life.

- For more **fun**: Define what fun means to you, and then find seven fun things, one that takes one minute, one that takes five minutes, one that takes ten minutes, one that takes 30 minutes, one that takes 45 minutes, one that takes 60 minutes, and one that takes two hours. Then pick one of your "fun things" and do a different one every day.

- For more **love**: Find whatever you respect about yourself, turn it into a positive statement, and make that be the first thing you say to yourself in your mind when you wake up each morning.

- For more **motivation**: Think back to something worthwhile that you've accomplished. Reflect upon the process you went through that created the success. Next, think of something you really want in your life and creatively apply that same process.

- For **reassurance**: Learn to say to yourself, *"I always do my best, and I am open to both reflection and learning how to be even better."*
- For **relaxation**: Take four deep breaths in and out—on a four count—and remind yourself that, *"This too shall pass."*
- For more **romance**: Appreciate yourself and all the things you do in your own life. Then uncover and know what makes you feel special, and be willing to communicate that to those closest to you.

Be Intentional

So many diets and eating plans give you the list of all that you **cannot** have. Over the course of the diet, all these restrictions typically leave people feeling constrained, limited, and unmotivated. The lack of motivation then creates laziness, which eventually leads to thoughts like, *"Forget this—I'm eating what I want."* That's why consciously becoming more intentional will assist you in making healthier choices, eating smaller portions, and—consequently—making you feel like you are actually giving up less.

"Those who fail to plan, plan to fail." This quote (said by many) is so true. When we don't act with intention or purpose, we get ourselves into trouble. Think back to the last time you were too tired to go to the grocery store. How did that decision affect your food choices that week? Did you stop at more fast food places, eat items in your fridge that were unsatisfying, or just simply feel a little more frustrated that week? Whatever the answer, the lesson is **intention creates peace** and, without, it you typically have chaos. The intention of going to the grocery store prepares you to have sensible, nourishing food throughout the week. When you have healthy food in your fridge, you naturally make more nutritious choices. Intention, therefore, becomes the obvious way to execute a plan, take action, and—ultimately—enjoy success.

When you learn to be intentional with your food choices, it becomes possible—and even easy—to only eat half! This is a gradual process and won't happen overnight but, when you put your intention into practice, you will see it pay off. Below are a couple of suggestions that you can apply that will help you become more intentional with food:

- Create and follow a plan.
- Go to the grocery store weekly, and plan all your meals ahead of time.
- Cook all your dinners on a free day or in one night, and then fridge and freeze portion sizes.
- When enjoying junk food, remember to eat three bites and chew them **slowly**.
- When eating out, only eat what is on the left side of your plate.
- Stay conscious with each and every bite.
- If you want to eat more, first answer the *Food Inquiry Questions*.

You don't ever have to give up what you love—you can still have it—but learn to:

1. *Taste the first three bites.*
2. *Stop using food to fill up your inner emptiness.*
3. *Be intentional about what you eat.*

To slim **the continuous appetite** find the hole that food is trying to fill, and give yourself what you actually desire.

—Inner-Query Six—

The World is Your Teacher

In this exercise you are asked to look at your current situation or circumstance as a teacher. While this can be a difficult perspective to come from, it can bring you tremendous growth. Once you grow you can usually move beyond your difficult situation, therefore, the result can be priceless! Please think of your most current challenging situation and follow these steps to see how *The World is Your Teacher*:

A. *Open your journal and ask the following questions to unlock the possible lesson on hand.*

1. *What is challenging to me about this situation?*

2. *What am I being asked to learn?*

3. *What have I learned through this experience?*

4. *How can I practice what I have learned in a positive way?*

B. *Take the answers and awareness you find and commit to remembering and practicing that new awareness, rather than replaying the old circumstance in your mind.*

If you found this exercise to be helpful,
please store it in your *Holistic Tool Box*.

—PART TWO—

Healing Your
Inner Issues

—Chapter 7—

The Power Within

*When you understand the tremendous power you
contain within, you simultaneously develop an incredible
authority over the continuous appetite.*

I t was a cold winter day. I was attending community college and
living at my parent's home in Princeton, New Jersey. One Thursday
afternoon, I had finished all my assigned schoolwork and I remember
sitting on the couch, glancing out the window and noticing how gray
it was outside. The next thing I knew, my head was in the refrigerator
and I was cramming turkey smeared with mayonnaise, chocolate and
peanuts into my mouth. It was like I had zoned out from my earlier
observation of the gray outdoors to that moment of overeating.

What happened? How did my face get smothered with mayo, my
mouth filled with melted chocolate, and my teeth packed with peanut
remnants? I immediately began to beat myself up mentally but, all of

a sudden, a thought surfaced and I remembered that I could follow a different approach to this overeating session.

At that moment, I stopped eating and grabbed three things: chewing gum, my journal and water. Then I moved fifty feet away from where I was eating, and began to face my demons and myself. In the next couple of moments, while I was journaling, I realized that something had been "off" in me way before I began eating, but the act of compulsively overeating is what got my attention to even pause, think, and write it out. I then began to backtrack through my day. I wrote about everything that had occurred, and then remembered a situation that happened earlier in the day.

A picture surfaced in my mind of a facial expression I'd received from one of my teachers. I had interpreted this look as the teacher saying, "Are you stupid?" I didn't consciously know how to digest the overwhelming unpleasant emotions that this expression triggered. I subconsciously just shoved those bad and hurt feelings down and went on with my day. I had been in the habit of "swallowing" down these unacknowledged emotions, but eventually they bubbled up, which negative feelings always do. And that's when—and why—I found myself eating.

I like to call this point "The Shift". We all have shifts throughout the day, and they can be as simple as a facial expression that triggers a childhood wound or as blatant as a verbal comment that breaks your heart. Whatever the situation, it's important to find "the shift" by looking back over the day to discover what has occurred that might trigger you to overeat. By implementing the simple effort of daily reflection, you can save yourself from succumbing to continuous eating.

When I reflected upon my day and understood that my teacher's facial expression had been the culprit for making me feel so bad, I was then able to analyze the incident. As a result, I had the following conversation with myself:

"Sophie, what happened earlier today?"

I asked my teacher a question and she looked at me like I was stupid.

"Did she say you were stupid?"

No, she just looked at me that way.

"So, if she did not say you were stupid, how do you know she was thinking that?"

*I **don't** know that she was thinking that. I just perceived her expression that way, and then I felt bad.*

"So then YOU felt that you were stupid?"

Yes.

"Does this feeling have anything to do with her?"

I guess it doesn't. I have always felt stupid, fat and ugly—from the time I was a little girl. And this "expression" came from a teacher, so I felt stupid. If I'd been at the gym, however, and received the same expression, I probably would've felt fat or, at a bar, I would've felt ugly.

"What does your teacher—or anyone else—have to do with these feelings?"

Other people trigger these feelings in me, and it has to do with my inner issue of feeling bad about myself.

"If other people trigger these feelings IN YOU, is it their fault?"

No. I need to take responsibility for my inner gunk and begin to look at things that feel bad or are "triggers" as a message to show me where I need to grow. I think that, with this approach, I feel empowered!

"Are you ready to grow?"

Yes.

"Well, you're right on track because the first part—acknowledgment— is done. The next step is looking for the truth. So what is your truth?"

The truth is that I'm extremely sensitive to feeling stupid, fat and ugly, and I've felt this way my whole life. I seem to interpret random people's expressions in a negative way. This, however, is not fair to them, because these feelings are MY issue. **I now see that I don't need to put the blame on others in order to understand my life lessons.**

For years, this "facial expression" experience had the power to send me into a bout of continuous eating. After journaling, however, I was able to see that **there is always a message behind the eating.**

Negative thoughts and actions can come from hidden issues you subconsciously have about your past, and these may have driven you to eat, which then left you feeling horrible about yourself. The problem, however, is the *pattern* of feeling bad about yourself. There may be many reasons why you can justify this "bad" feeling but, when it's all said and done, feeling bad comes from hidden inner issues of the past. The way out of this pattern is to reflect through journaling and look for the ways you may be contributing to the situation.

Unresolved Issues Need an Outlet

Thought is one of the quickest and most powerful energies we have. When we have unresolved inner issues, we tend to create an outlet to release energy. Outlets arrive through external situations and relationships. Our unsettled issues are sitting behind the scene of these circumstances and, in essence, are waiting for a release. Therefore, we attract situations to us that allow us to express this troubled energy. Our subconscious knows what we need to release and is able to relinquish this energy on these situations. Simply put, what goes in (emotionally or otherwise) must come out.

In the story above, I had been hurt by a simple facial expression because of what was already inside **me**. No one else can make you feel stupid, fat or ugly, because these emotions are within **you**. A person may **trigger** these thoughts and feelings within, but it is important to remember that this inner experience is your own gunk. Once you embrace that concept, you'll have the power to change it.

The teacher could have been thinking, *"Oops, I forgot to change the laundry,"* and may not even have been listening to me. My unaddressed inner issues, however, led me to perceive the experience as an insult which I took personally, and the result was that I felt bad about myself. The issue, deep down, was that I'd always felt bad about myself, and feeling stupid, fat or ugly were just symptoms of this deep, inner hurt. One lesson I took away from all of this was: **If I continue to feel bad about myself on the inside, I will continue to attract situations that help me release this awful feeling.**

There is, however, a way out and it is—once again—through awareness. Please practice opening your journal, asking yourself reflective questions about your day, and then backtrack through your earlier experiences to find where you may be stuffing down unacknowledged emotions. Next, it is important to comprehend that you will have to generally acknowledge and experience these feelings in order to overcome them. Therefore, when the feelings surface, know that you are okay, and that allowing yourself to experience them is part of the process to healing your inner issues.

When these emotions surface, your assignment is to make a commitment to face yourself for the next five minutes. Say to yourself, *"I commit to NOT eating anything for the next five minutes, and instead I will do some inner work. I will open my journal, ask **The Four Questions**, and be with myself. Then, when my five minutes are up, I will drink eight ounces of water and—if I truly need to—I will only eat one serving of something that I desire."*

Not surprisingly, if you start practicing a different response to these feelings, you will end up having a different outcome. If you continue to get the idea to eat, I encourage you to stop whatever you are doing and go into a quiet space. For example, if you're at work, a party, your family's or friend's house, school—or wherever—, go into the bathroom. Once you get away from all the distractions you can ask yourself, *"What am I feeling?"* Once you have found the source of your inner suffering, you can ask yourself if you are ready to leave that place, and then choose to leave by asking yourself what it is you DO want.

Look for a new awareness and try to deal with what comes to mind. Ask yourself if other feelings are connected to what you DO want—feelings that you can choose **now**. Then ask yourself how you can give yourself whatever it is that you truly want. The final step is to silence the chatter, come into this very moment, and then activate your inner power!

After you start taking the time to stop and be with yourself, you may notice that some of your inner issues will begin to surface in daily situations. These issues, however, are your past painful experiences that are resurfacing to help you grow. In the past, you may not have had the much-needed resources to help you embrace the situation in an insightful way, which had the counterproductive result of shoving the experience down. Remember that *what comes in must come out* so, if you do the inner work and let it come out in an organized manner, these issues will be transformed into wise inner treasures that can make your life sparkle.

Thoughts Create Things

Your life is a physical manifestation of the thoughts, feelings and beliefs that you predominantly hold inside. There is an energy force—between all objects—that draws them together, and you're currently attracting what you think about most. Whatever you are focusing on, even if it is something you do not want, this is what will show up in your life. Why is this? Because, when we focus our thoughts on any (one) thing, we are placing and pulsing energy around that idea. This then attracts a **similar** energy to help it manifest.

Thought is creation, and a great first step in gaining more awareness over your body, emotions, mind, and spiritual experience is by looking at your current reality to see what you have created.

Look at your life and see what is around you. Generally speaking, does it feel good or does it feel bad? Whatever you see is a direct reflection of what your thoughts and feelings have focused on. This may be hard to swallow and you may feel as if you didn't attract the car accident, your difficult boss, domineering parents, an illness, skin problems, weight issues, or whatever the issue is that you feel is a stain on your life. But, once you embrace that your life is a physical manifestation of the thoughts, feelings and beliefs that you predominantly hold inside, you can actually begin to recognize the power you have within to change your life.

When I began to recognize how my thoughts were creating things, I first saw how off-track I was from where I wanted to be. First, I recognized that my initial thoughts were, *"Oh my goodness, I cannot deal with what is happening in my life!"* Under the surface, I constantly expressed this thought, which then triggered the emotion of anxiety and panic. This "thought and anxiety cycle" then created an avalanche of experiences that left me feeling anxious about everything that happened, which always led me right into the kitchen.

If we can see where we are, we can make a conscious choice to move away from that place. If your mind has been focusing (consciously or unconsciously) on negative and defeating thoughts, then this is what will arrive in your life. Once you become aware of what your mind is thinking and notice the parts that are predominantly negative, you can then reflect and look for the opposite of that thought. After you find the opposite, concentrate on it, feel it with intention, and watch that new focus begin to manifest in your life.

When I noticed that I ultimately felt bad about myself (which appeared as feeling stupid, fat and ugly), I then knew where I authentically stood within myself and had a foundation to stand on. Next, I asked myself if I was ready to leave this place of suffering and then explored what I really wanted. I realized that I wanted to feel attractive, fit, and intelligent. These were the opposite of those bad feelings and negative images. These were positive thoughts, and they felt so good that I began to practice these feelings and recited them to myself on a daily basis. Eventually, I started to believe them, and then I became what I had envisioned.

Positive thought is infinitely more powerful than a negative thought. So **the act of recognizing what feels bad and then changing those thoughts to what feels good will strengthen and change your life in ways you can't even imagine.** Everything you feel in your heart is the whisper of your ultimate purpose and, in this lifetime, you can have whatever you want. When you feel good, you are on track. If, however, you tend to feel bad, it is an indication that you may need to take the time to discover:

- what you have been thinking about
- what you truly want
- how you can begin to pursue and possess what you want

Visualization

Once you begin to get in touch with what it is you DO want, visualization is a great way to bring that energy to you. Have you ever been listening to a great storyteller and actually *see* the picture he or she is describing? Sometimes, it can seem so vivid that it actually *feels* like you're there. This is your mind's eye, your imagination, your thoughts creating a picture. It's called **visualization**.

Visualization is the act of forming a clear visual image or picture of something that you want in your mind. It is a powerful tool to fuse together your imagination and the power of the mind. There are many types of visualization, and I am going to describe two forms: **reflective visualization** and **meditative visualization**. Both of these exercises can be done in a quiet, calm space whenever you have at least fifteen minutes of uninterrupted time to yourself. Please read through the following sequences and see which one you prefer. Next, go into your quiet space, and place this book on your lap so, if necessary, you can refer to the directions as you practice.

Reflective Visualization

Enter your calm, quiet and safe space. Close your eyes, become still within, center yourself, and quiet your chatter. Sit back and feel yourself come into your body. Take a couple of deep breaths on a four count (four counts in, four counts out.) Next, identify what emotion you are experiencing in this moment. Imagine and then visualize the emotion as someone at the front door, wanting to come inside. Stop and spend a moment with this image. Next, answer the door. Ask, *"How can I help you? What is your name? What are you doing here? Who sent you?"* Pause and wait for an answer and trust whatever answers come up. (Note: Try not to feel silly, because this exercise can really help you confront your inner fears.) After you have received some information and feel you have had enough, take a couple of deep breaths. Do not just open your eyes and come out of this reflective state but, instead, honor your inner life and leave the scene in a respectful way. After you have heard or given this inner fear a name, you now know specially who and what you are dealing with. Consequently, if the emotion surfaces in the future, you will know what you are dealing with and how to write about it in your journal. The point of this visualization is to reclaim your power and realize that **you** are in charge, not your fears. It's now time to acknowledge and reclaim your power.

Meditative Visualization

Again, enter your calm, quiet and safe space. Close your eyes, become still within, center yourself, and quiet your chatter. Sit back and feel yourself come into your body. Take a couple of deep breaths on a four count (four counts in, four counts out). Start by imagining something you would like to manifest. In this moment, pick one goal to work with. As Shatki Gawain (author of CREATIVE VISUALIZATION) says, create a vivid, positive mental picture in your mind's eye, incorporating as many details as you can.

There are no limits to this. Your visualization could be a different career, a healing of your body, your perfect home, an object desired, your life's purpose, a rewarding relationship, a situation, or whatever it is that happens to be in your heart. Focus on what it feels like to already have this and deeply inquire, "*What does it look like? What does it feel like? What emotions come to the surface as I have this?*" Imagine yourself as being, experiencing, and having this (whatever it is) **now**. See yourself in this mental picture. Be one with it.

Next, sit with this image for five minutes and surround those thoughts with all your positive energy. Be with this picture as it is happening now. When you feel the session is naturally coming to an end, surround your image in a bubble, let go of the bubble, and then see that bubble float away from you. This is the act of releasing your image so it has the ability to go and collect all the energy it needs to bring it to manifestation.

Now it is time to come back. Take a couple of deep breaths and gradually bring yourself back into the moment. Let go and release this experience. Open your eyes and quietly say, *"I trust that I am in synergy with whatever it is that I want. I embrace that the manifestation will be the best outcome for me and all concerned."*

Review of The Daily Basics

The Daily Basics are the first exercises outlined in Chapter 1, and they are the foundation for your healing. These exercises are what will continually improve your body's health, your emotional awareness, your mental state and your spiritual connection. Doing *The Daily Basics* is like taking a shower in the morning and getting clean and ready for the day by washing off all of the residue from yesterday. Our inner life also needs a "cleansing shower" and *The Daily Basics* is the perfect way to clean the inner self. Here's the foundation:

❖ Get a journal, and write for five minutes about whatever is on your mind.

❖ Answer the *Inner Refresher Questions* to tune in to yourself:

1. *What sensations do I feel in my body today?*
2. *What am I feeling right now?*
3. *What am I thinking about?*
4. *What does my spiritual connection feel like today?*

❖ Quiet the mind, and sit in silence for ten minutes per day.

❖ Make a list of five things that you are thankful for, with no repeats!

The next step is to ad in a couple of new components:

- Take ten deep breaths a day (on a four count in and out).
- Drink half of your body weight in ounces of water per day.
- Look into the mirror for one minute, smile and say *"I Love You."*
- Spend five minutes per day with a relaxation technique that works for you and most important, relax your face.

As you practice the exercises at your own pace, you will transform. Please know that facing yourself requires a great amount of courage. This process of healing takes tremendous strength, and I commend you in your journey thus far. When you understand the tremendous power you contain within, you simultaneously develop an incredible authority over **the continuous appetite**.

The Opposite Emotion Chart

This exercise is designed to expand your emotional awareness and language. It will help you see how many emotions there are, and how you can begin to truly tune in to yourself and find what you are actually feeling.

A. *Take a blank sheet of lined paper and draw a vertical line down the middle.*

B. *Then name the two columns at the top: LOVE and FEAR.*

C. *Next, begin to think of all the emotions that come to mind and write them down in the proper column, but leave a space on the opposite row (so that, later, you can find the opposite emotion).*

D. *Now, write the opposite emotion in the other column, but only write down an emotion once.*

E. *Try to get about 20 emotions on each side.*

Example Chart

Love	Fear
Happiness	
	Anger
Joy	
	Frustration
	Rejection

If you found this exercise to be helpful, please store it in your *Holistic Tool Box*.

—Chapter 8—

A New Perspective

*Affirmations will weed out the past influence of the continuous appetite
by planting new thoughts that blossom into a pleasant reality.*

To deliberately create great things in your life, it's crucial to become aware of the three levels of the mind: **Chatter, Cognition,** and **The Now**. These three levels can be compared to a garden where the chatter is a weed, the cognition is a plant, and the now is a blossoming flower. When we look at the mind as a landscape, we can see how the random chattering thoughts act as weeds that steal all the nutrients from the soil.

A plant without nutrition will not blossom and, in the same way, a thought without clarity can neither flourish nor function. Therefore, this shows us how important it is to silence those useless thoughts and pluck those ugly weeds. This act will allow the soil (your brain) to replenish itself, which results in a better, clearer thinking process.

The whole point of thinking is to find solutions but, if you have a weed growing in between each of your thoughts, it can be difficult to have clear insights that help create positive solutions. In order to authentically transform your perspective, it's essential to:

- practice silencing your chatter
- find solutions from your cognition
- consciously choose to live in the now

Silencing Your Chatter

As previously discussed in Chapter One, chatter is that string of random sentences that pop into your thinking from nowhere, and are usually meaningless. Chatter is a weed in your mind, and now is the time to become aware of when and how to pluck the weed from the garden. Hopefully, you have begun to develop an awareness of this rambling voice and have also practiced ways to silence it. Before we go further, let's take a moment to renew the process by which you'll accomplish this.

In order to remove the weeds from your mind, you'll need to be aware of: 1) what your chatter sounds like, 2) when it happens, and 3) how to command it to stop, which is done through a simple "shush". Over time, the chatter will follow your command, at first fluctuating from loud and fast to soft and quiet, then growing to full volume again. This is when you simply need to stay dedicated to the "shush" and silence it! As this process is continually practiced, the chatter will eventually be disabled.

If you are chattering about tasks or things that you need to get done for the day, bring a notebook with you to write down the necessary information and get it off your mind. Often, one task that is repeated again and again in your mind can feel like ten different directions.

However, the moment that you write the task down and get it off your mind, you'll feel a soothing sense of mental empowerment.

Remember, the information that is passed at this level will not help you be more productive or efficient. It's actually quite the opposite because chatter takes away from whatever is happening in real time, right now. Once the chatter is silenced, you can easily enter the next level of the mind where you can think clearly. This next level is **cognition**.

Finding Cognitive Solutions

Cognition is the thought process of the mind. It's where you acquire knowledge, attain a new perspective, solve problems logically and, most important, create solutions. This level of the mind can be compared to the beautiful plants in a garden. The ultimate goal of your cognition is to have a clear thinking process, which leads you to finding solutions.

Many people use their mind deliberately forty hours a week or more but, when the chatter is too active, it prevents the discovery of solutions, or the growth and enjoyment of healthy plants. Without solutions, you may feel stuck and overwhelmed with a current task or a problem that you have been assigned to solve. The whole point of cognition is to ultimately create solutions, so the mind can have a break. At the most simplistic level, your mind is the trouble-shooting center of your life. Therefore, it needs to be able to function at an optimal level.

When you continually silence your mental chatter, it will definitely lose its power. As the result, mental clarity can help you then begin to look for a solution to the current thought or task. Through this approach, you will find that you start to effectively see how to create solutions to the problems that complicate your life. When you have a solution-oriented mind frame, you'll begin to feel more balanced, peaceful, and rested.

The next step is to begin to probe even deeper and ask, *"How is this situation asking me to grow?"* The answer to this question will then unlock a new perspective that has the potential to release you from the past. This solution-oriented mind frame, or calmed mental state will supply a sense of relief that feels good, and can take you to the third level of the mind: **The Now.**

Living in The Now

The Now is a place of stillness and serenity, and could ideally be where your whole life happens. For me, **The Now** is where peace and God exist. Just for this moment, I want you to stop and look around. Take a deep breath and notice all the things that surround you. Are there grenades flying through the air or angry people banging on your door? No, probably not. Life, however, can sometimes feel that way when you first come out of your chatter.

To continue with the analogy of the garden, **The Now** is compared to the blossom that comes from a healthy plant. When we silence the chatter and create solutions through our thinking, we can then learn to transition into the perpetual peacefulness of **The Now**.

Right now, this exact moment—before you even think about it—is The Now, and entering it is a simple choice that comes after you have shut off the chatter and found solutions by using your clear thinking process. Entering this space will immediately help you feel that everything is okay right now, and it will allow you to see that anytime you do not feel okay, it's usually because your mind is chattering without seeking viable solutions.

When I first came into **The Now**, I felt as if I had left a war zone. I had a war going on inside my head which felt like grenades were flying at me and people were chasing me. But, in reality, it was all just a feeling created through my own flawed thinking, and I hadn't even been conscious that is was happening. Once I began to practice the three simple steps of 1) silencing the Chatter, 2) finding solutions through my clear Cognition, and then 3) consciously choosing to live in The Now, I experienced a place of peace that I'd never before known possible.

The Now is a space that is peaceful and calm. Even if you have witnessed a tragedy or been in a car accident, the actual time of those events in reality (**The Now**) is merely seconds. In one lifetime, you may only collectively experience a couple of minutes of misfortune. The brain, however, can replay those scenarios and rerun the pictures over and over again in your mind, which—obviously—leaves you feeling bad. Once again, this is the chattering mind, and it needs to be silenced.

In life, there is always a certain amount of suffering and pain but, out of every painful situation, comes an opportunity. I'm not suggesting that you don't have to process tragedies and grieve over loss, as these behaviors are part of being emotionally balanced. What I am saying is that you don't have to replay the unusable scenarios over and over again in your mind to prolong feeling bad. Instead, look for the hidden opportunity in every situation, and view it as a chance to grow.

When we silence the chatter (remove the weeds) and find solutions through a clear thinking process (grow a healthy plant), the mind is then set up to come into **The Now** (a blossoming flower). Once the garden is in this condition, all your thoughts will blossom into their greatest destiny, and you can consciously choose to live a more peaceful life.

Guilt is the Messenger

Guilt is a messenger that is in your life to take you on an educational journey. Many people, however, live as if guilt is the destination. Feeling guilty can be painful, but pain is God's megaphone trying to get your attention to make a different choice.

When I first confessed my eating issues to my mom on that Easter Sunday back in 2001, I was swimming in a sea of guilt, a sea so deep that I was beginning to drown, but I didn't even know it. I felt guilty over everything, from the healthy or unhealthy food I put into my mouth, to the things I said to people, to the choices I made. It was rare that I didn't feel guilty. The feeling of guilt typically felt like I had done something wrong, but what is wrong with eating lunch, speaking my mind, or making choices? My guilt receptor was way off and I needed God's help to get it back on track.

Once I became aware that excessive and counterproductive guilt was one of my surfacing problems, I began to release it to God by reciting, *"God, I release this guilt to you and ask that you fill me with purity."* The first week, I must have said this little prayer six hundred times a day. The next week, however, I was down to about one hundred. The following week, I was down to about fifty and by the fourth week, I can remember only saying it five to ten times a day. The residual effect from this exercise not only gave me a life jacket to use while floating in the sea of guilt; eventually, it pulled me out and dried me off. It's like the cloud of guilt had been lifted from my heart, and I was able to see more clearly.

When it comes to guilt, I encourage you to embrace a new perspective and be willing to release it to God. As I let go of my guilt, I began to see how the guilt-driven emotions that surfaced were really carrying a strong message. When I got too caught up in the feeling of powerlessness, however, I wasn't able to identify the lesson. After I had released it to God, within about a month, I began to see the message behind it.

I felt guilty for eating food because, deep down, I was out of synergy with what being healthy truly meant, and food became a way that I beat myself up. I felt guilty about speaking my mind because I always felt that, if I spoke up, someone would see through me. I felt guilty because I had complicated inner issues that needed to be healed and, once that guilt was slightly lifted, I was able to heal the true issue.

The most important thing to remember is that you have done—up until this point—what you needed to do in order to survive, but it is now time to LIVE. I encourage you to transform your relationship with guilt by reflecting upon the situation at hand and follow this process:

1. *Notice when your guilt surfaces.*
2. *Recite a powerful affirmation to God, releasing your guilt.*
3. *Make a commitment to let the guilt go.*
4. *Welcome the opportunity for guilt to show you a deeper message.*

Guilt can be your teacher, and life can be your classroom. Your goal is to have the feeling of guilt become a trigger for you to evaluate, expand, and learn. As you accept and learn to follow this process, you'll transform your inner issues, change your life perspective, and begin to reap the reward of all your hard work.

Transformational Thinking

I believe in transformational thinking, which is an element of positive thinking, but NOT the cliché of "positive thinking". I have heard countless people say, "I need to have a more positive outlook on life and think more positive thoughts." Most people think that "positive thinking" means to cover up their negativity with positivity, but this is like trying to paint over a hole in the wall. While the paint might camouflage the hole, it cannot repair the hole. Instead, you need to *renovate* your negative feelings and *transform* them into positive ones.

Being positive is a transformational experience that requires real honesty. In order to transform your thinking, it's crucial to first become truthful and straightforward regarding your deep negative thoughts. Then, be willing to do the inner work by taking five minutes to ask *The Four Questions* (*1. What happened today? 2. What emotion was I feeling? 3. What does this feel like within? 4. What do I want to feel?*), dissect your negative feelings, thoughts, or situations, and ultimately discover what it is you DO want. The final step is to help your mind see the quickest path to reaching your goals, and that is through affirmations.

Affirmations

The mind—which is not limited to the brain, but rather acts as the floating command center—delivers its instructions through thought. Thought then sends a message to your system to notice the very thing that you desire. For example, *"I am fat"* sends poison down through the system, and the instructions are clear: *"Only notice everything that I want to eat that makes me feel bad and fat."* When you transform this affirmation into, *"I am beautiful,"* the mind unlocks everything in the command center to make this happen, and the mind begins to say, *"Do you hear that? Unlock the beauty; it's time to heal!"* Turn your individual desires—which are important because they are whispers from God that are planted within—into affirmations to help you achieve your ultimate purpose.

An affirmation is a positive statement of support or agreement. We are affirming most of the time, whether we realize it or not. Therefore, it's in our best interest to learn how to effectively use this powerful tool. An affirmation is like a road in your mind, and a positive affirmation can be compared to a drive down a beautiful road. Often, we allow ourselves to spend time in bad neighborhoods within our thinking, and don't even realize that we are there. We do not have to continue to drive down these negative paths, and affirmations are the road maps that will lead us out.

The correct way to create an affirmation is to first acknowledge what you are thinking or feeling, then look for what you *want* to think and feel and (finally) convert that desire into a positive statement or affirmation. It is important to remember that all affirmations are born from a former place of weakness within you that you must acknowledge in order to release. To achieve this you must:

1. *First, acknowledge your inner weakness.*
2. *Next, think about what it was that you truly want.*
3. *Finally, turn that negative feeling or past experience into a positive affirmation.*

Here is an example of how you can take one simple thought and transform it into a positive affirmation. For instance, I felt disgusted with myself. Here is the process that the thought went through: 1) acknowledgement ("I feel disgusted with myself"), 2) I asked myself what I want ("I want to love myself") and, 3) I transformed it into a positive statement ("I love you, Sophie"). Here are some more examples:

1) I hate myself. → *2) I want to like myself.* → *3) I accept myself.*
1) I feel full of anxiety. → *2) I want to feel better.* → *3) I remain calm.*
1) I don't have enough. → *2) I want to be more giving.* → *3) I am generous.*

Some other affirmations include: *I am at peace with others. I allow God's goodness to flow through my life. I feel God with me, always. I am of great value to this world and others. I always have enough for myself and for others. I create all that I desire. My thoughts, words and actions are in harmony. I am at peace with others.*

When creating affirmations, it's important to use the words: *I am, I have,* and *I embrace.* This shows your mind where you are going with no speed bumps to slow you down. Next, you want to stay away from statements that use the words: *I want, I will,* or *I hope.* While these statements can seem positive, they are the middle step to creating an affirmation and leave you feeling the "want" instead of the "have".

You might wonder, *"How do I believe that I can **have** these things when they seem so far away or unrealistic?"* The answer is through faith. I believe we want the things that are somehow tied to our destiny, and we need to have faith in God, ourselves, and the process to ultimately realize our goals and dreams. Faith is the deep inner belief that **one day you will see it**. It is the step before you see it because, once you see it, there is no more need for faith.

Getting in touch with what you DO want is the first step in creating powerful affirmations. The next step is to write down twenty affirmations and begin to recite them to yourself every day. Observe how you feel when you say them because you want to feel uplifted and empowered, so if you feel bad at any point, edit the affirmation until you have a good feeling while saying it.

Your muscles grow through repetition, and your mind is like a muscle. It needs to practice, work out, and repeat in order to remember the new road you're trying to create. Start by repeating your affirmations for at least five minutes per day. You can get creative with how you practice your affirmations. You might want to record your voice saying these affirmative statements on your cell phone and then listen to them, or you can try writing them on index cards and keeping them in your wallet. You can even place sticky notes where you spend a lot of time.

As you explore and discover what it is you DO want, your future experiences will seem to reflect a more positive path, and a healthier perspective toward life will emerge. Affirmations will weed out the past influence of **the continuous appetite** by planting new thoughts that blossom into a pleasant reality.

—Inner-Query Eight—

The Power of Affirmations

Affirmations are a positive statement of support or agreement toward what it is you desire. When writing your affirmations, pay attention to how you feel and make sure they make you feel uplifted. To see a result from your affirmative work, practice with repetition for about 12 weeks and you will see them begin to manifest.

A. *Take out a loose sheet of paper.*

B. *Write down everything you want.*

C. *Turn that "I want" statement into an "I have," "I am," or "I embrace" statement.*

D. *Use a 3 x 5 card and write one affirmation per card.*

E. *Keep these cards with you and practice repeating them to yourself for five minutes per day.*

Sample Affirmations:

- *"Everything is OK right now."*
- *"I am filled with positive energy."*
- *"My body is healthy."*
- *"I can handle change."*
- *"God is with me right now."*

If you found this exercise to be helpful, please store it in your *Holistic Tool Box.*

—Chapter 9—

Why Things Happen

When you see pain as a messenger, life circumstances have more significance and the continuous appetite finally loses its power over you.

What happens to you in life is not as important as how you choose to handle it. Most situations in our current reality do not have the power to hurt us today, but many of us subconsciously fester in our pain from the *past*. This then creates a reaction, which can cause a conflict in our present. The goal then becomes to observe your reactions to find *the issues hiding behind the pain* and to ultimately use this pain as information regarding where you need to heal.

Do you know the difference between a reaction and a response? In the simplest terms, the only difference is that a reaction comes **before** thought, and a response comes **after** a conscious thought. When we have issues from the past that get in our way, it's common to react inappropriately to the present. This is just one more way that **the continuous appetite** can bite you in the butt.

Did you know that another basic difference between reacting and responding is that they are only separated from each other by three seconds? But these three seconds are crucial, because they create a space. There is, of course, a space that exists within all communication, but most people are unaware of this because their mind is chattering. In that important space, you can then choose to consciously think about what is truly unfolding in your circumstance and what would be your most appropriate response. This means that, if you can pause and count to three, you enter the space where you can actually think before you react, and this is the first step to transitioning into responding.

When you truly begin to tune in and listen when you're communicating with others, you'll become more aware of this space. This space then creates room for conscious thought and, from there, choice is activated and your cravings can be controlled.

It's Your Choice

When you go out to a restaurant, you're given a menu that shows you what the restaurant offers. From those options, you narrow it down to what you want to eat and then order that. Believe it or not, life gives us a menu as well. You may not be able to see it, but this menu typically appears through difficult situations. Why? Because *humans rarely grow when things are easy.* Life then provides us with a precious human gift called **choice**.

Many people struggle with making choices, but one opportunity that only humans have is the ability to truly choose what it is they want in life. Now is the time to learn how to become a great "choice maker" by implementing a three-pronged simple act.

To make the best choice possible, you must first think it, feel it, and go with it. If "it"—your choice—does not work out, the experience can then teach you a lesson. The bottom line is that we need to learn lessons in this life, and there is no way around it. These lessons then create self-growth, which usually comes through uncomfortable and unlikeable conditions. Often, challenge brings strength and pain brings growth. The good news is that the result of these lessons helps us make better choices in the future.

I believe that self-growth is a major part of our destiny here on Earth, and it is what needs to happen in order for the "item chosen" off the "menu of life" to be delivered. I once heard someone (I think it was Oprah) say that, when you are able to look back at the things that once beat you up in life and can be grateful that they happened, it means that you have truly healed. Your struggle with food has so many insightful messages to deliver you and I trust that, one day, you will choose to be on the other side of this "food fight". This result will come from a series of choices that you have probably already begun to make. So keep going and remember that every choice you make really matters.

The Rule of Three

"Why do bad things happen?" "Why can't I just lose this weight, get the job, or have more money right now?" "Why do I need to go through this?" The general answer to all these questions is simple. **Things happen to you in order to help you grow into your greatest self.**

In life, we are continually provided with ups and downs, the good and bad, and the dark and light. These dualities, however, have a deeper message behind them and, when we take the time to seek out what we are being asked to learn, we can receive the message that life is trying to deliver. Sometimes things happen that seem to be from left field, and my goal is to help you find the meaning behind your circumstance.

As I went through the process of healing *my* continuous appetite, I had to face a lot of difficult things that had happened in my past. They were hard to face, but the process eventually gave me great wisdom. As I faced my inner darkness, there were many times that I would ask, *"Why can't I just lose this weight?"* That frustrating question alone made me suffer. What I didn't know at the time was that there were lessons attached to every pound I wanted to lose—all seventy-five of them! I learned that in order to truly let go of the weight, I'd have to really face myself and that, once I said YES to this process, it was not as scary as I once (subconsciously) feared. Once I really looked at my demons in the closet, it was as if they had lost most of their power and I was then able to learn **the lesson behind the weight** and replace that pain with awareness and healing.

I was carrying a curriculum of self-awareness within my extra weight and once I began to see that, I was able to learn the lessons (slowly). The result was that the weight gradually melted away! My total weight loss occurred over an eight-year period (so when I say slow, I mean SLOW), and one of the reasons I know this weight will not come back is because the issue which was attached to each and every pound has been healed.

As I was learning my lessons, I fell upon an awareness that made my life circumstances so much easier to digest. I realized that there are three reasons why things might happen:

1. *It is an answered prayer in disguise.*
2. *It is the Law of Attraction manifesting.*
3. *It is a life lessons that we need to learn to help us fulfill our purpose.*

A single situation can predominantly be one of these items or a blend of all three. This awareness gave me a road map to help me understand both where I was going and what I might be asked to learn. Here are some other examples:

David's Disguise

David wanted to make more money. He was earning a teacher's salary and was barely getting by. He had the habit of spending more than he made because he grew up in a household that always spent whatever they made, and he never learned to live within his means. As his debt grew, he cried out to God one night, *"God please help me, I want to make more money!"*

What David did not know at the time was that, in two years, he would have his dream job—a career in finance—which would require him to make significant and vital financial decisions for the well-being of the business. In order to excel at this, he would need to learn money management at the personal level first. After he cried out to God, he received a strong indication that he needed to put together a budget and follow it.

During the next two years, David learned to spend less than he made, got his personal spending habits under control, and gained more financial confidence. Then, one day, a parent of one of his students was speaking to him about an opportunity to work in finance and, right then and there, he knew that this was his dream job!

David applied, was interviewed, and landed a job which tripled his salary. His story is the classic scenario of a current circumstance that might be an **answer to prayer in disguise**, but it's up to you to find the camouflaged lesson. The moral of David's story is: look at your circumstances as an **opportunity to grow**. It might just be an answer to one of your prayers, now appearing in disguise. Once you have grown, however, you will be able to see how the painful circumstance has led to the necessary growth which ultimately leads to success.

Alice's Attraction

Alice wanted to lose weight. She had been carrying an extra twenty pounds since her last pregnancy—four years ago—and she wanted to drop it once and for all. What Alice didn't realize was that over the past four years, her mind had been continually beating her up over her weight gain. A normal conversation in Alice's head sounded like, *"I'm so fat and ugly; no one likes me or thinks I'm pretty anymore. I can't believe what I've done to myself. Who even cares about how I look? That piece of cake will make me feel better right now."* This dialogue was causing Alice to see herself in a negative way, which took away all her motivation to lose weight.

Alice then recognized that she was having a dreadful and non-motivating conversation with herself day in and day out. She began to see how this attitude had begun to attract certain counterproductive feelings, situations, and thoughts. She didn't like this at all and immediately began to take responsibility for her inner gunk which was causing this awful mental conversation and consequently drawing negative circumstances to her, which ultimately allowed her to release that horrible gunk within.

This is what the **Law of Attraction** does. It allows you to let out what you hold inside. Once Alice recognized that she needed to stop this negative conversation and turn it around, she was then willing and ready to change it. The next thing Alice did was write down all the things she was displeased with both about her body and life. She got all her negativity out onto paper, and then transformed it all into positive affirmation. She then made the commitment to stop thinking negative thoughts about herself, and instead recited her affirmations for thirty minutes a day. A week later, one of her friends invited her to a Weight

Watchers meeting, and she ended up joining. Alice faithfully followed the points program, and lost twenty pounds in three months!

The moral of Alice's story is that our minds do play a big role in our reality, and it's up to us to recognize this. When you have something in your life that you don't want, it's time to take a look at what your mind is dialoguing or chattering about that you might not be in touch with. Next, it's time to change it. The Law of Attraction is simple: **what you think about needs an outlet, and that outlet will draw circumstances to you that allow you to release that mental focus**. Once you know what you are mentally creating, you can create something different, something that you want!

Leslie's Lesson

Leslie was not happy with her roommate situation and didn't understand why she always had to live with such difficult and messy people. She was a producer, made a substantial living, but had the pattern of not speaking up for herself. She typically went along with what others wanted, which always led her right into another situation with a roommate who, in fact, pushed all her buttons.

The last straw came when she arrived home after a twenty-hour day, and the condo was a complete mess cluttered with dirty laundry and dishes, and reeking like an NFL locker room. That was the end of the rope for Leslie, and she flipped out. In a rage, she screamed at her roommate, *"I CAN'T TAKE THIS ANYMORE! YOU ARE SUCH A MESS. CLEAN THIS PLACE UP NOW!"* She then shouted, *"THAT'S IT, I'M MOVING AT THE END OF THE MONTH."* Leslie ran to her room, feeling overwhelmed and embarrassed about how she'd reacted, but then she remembered to get out her journal and face herself.

As she began to write out her frustrations about the dirty apartment, how it made her feel, and all that she had tolerated up to that point, she had an awareness. Leslie was suddenly aware that she felt a little relief from having told her roommate that the messy condo bothered her and, although she wasn't proud of the way she'd done it, something did feel better. It then dawned on her that she felt better because she'd spoken up for what she wanted.

One of Leslie's issues was that she never spoke up for herself. She would just take it and take it and take it, and then BLOW! By the time she blew, it was usually too late for any kind of reconciliation.

Through this situation, Leslie discovered that she had the pattern of holding her truth inside, so she made the decision to begin to speak up more. She then started to address the issues as to why she never spoke up, and her list included that she'd never seen a woman speak up articulately, she didn't know that it was okay to want what she wanted, and she felt uncomfortable with the idea of being rebuffed or rejected if she spoke up.

After she acknowledged all these inner statements, she immediately began to see that she no longer needed to hold onto these former restrictions, which led her to create a new set of rules to live by. The first rule was: **know how you feel, know what you want, and then articulately communicate that information to others.** Leslie then apologized to her roommate about her rage, which led to a conversation about order and cleanliness within the house. Her remorseful roommate really wanted to become cleaner and better organized. Through their conversation, they decided to develop house rules. They are now living happily together in a cleaner and more orderly home.

The moral to Leslie's story is that she had a **life lesson** to learn, which was to speak up for herself. Up to this point in her life, she simply had not truly understood that lesson. The way she knew it was a life lesson was because: 1) it empowered her after she went through it, 2) this information would be useful for the rest of her life, and 3) she saw how not learning this lesson had negatively affected her up to this point.

The life lessons each of us need to learn are all different, and are taught to us individually. But the most important thing to remember is that **life lessons are here to help you fulfill your purpose.**

I encourage you to use *The Rule of Three* next time you find yourself in any predicament. This technique will empower you to ensure a different perspective on your life conditions, and will then help you pull your own power back into your life.

A Deeper Meaning to Pain

When you are in pain, it's as if everything in your life becomes blurry, and nothing seems to matter as much as the pain. Pain can seem to come from nowhere and feel so overpowering that you can forget who you are, what your goals are, and what you believe in. Nevertheless, I encourage you to begin to look for a deeper meaning to pain of any caliber. Look inside your BEMS, as it has information attached to it which can assist you on your healing journey.

The body has a great indicator system which allows us to know when something is **off-center** or **out of balance**. This indictor system is called **pain**, and it gets our attention. Pain is an interesting thing that happens to the body when something is (consciously or unconsciously) left unattended to or unnoticed. Sometimes you may have emotional, mental, or spiritual issues that have been avoided and buried. These inner issues can then turn into a physical manifestation of blocked energy, which you will experience as pain.

We have all felt physical pain before, perhaps as an ache, discomfort, infection, or throbbing of some area. **Emotional** pain can be a current heartbreak, or a reaction from the past that hurts your present. **Mental** pain could be the constant analyzing, criticizing, judging, or thinking that makes you feel tired and drained. **Spiritual** pain (which most people are not even aware of) tends to feel like dread toward life, a lack of hope, or a general longing for connection. As I was releasing pain from my body, I began to see a pattern:

- Aching represents an unresolved stale issue.
- Gnawing pains represent an issue underneath the surface that's ready to be unlocked.
- Shooting pains represent a recent issue that needs to be worked through.
- Tightness represents anger that you might be holding onto.

No matter what type of pain you're feeling, if you take just a few minutes to journal and ask what the message is behind the pain, you'll receive an answer. Pain can actually empower you to look deeper into your inner life, leading you to receive the lesson you are being asked to learn. Once you become conscious of the idea that pain can be carrying a message, you can release a lot of stale hurt and—consequently—prevent it from coming into your future.

The Energy Centers

The body has seven different energy centers, called the chakras, which sit down the midline of the body and are psychosomatically connected to our BEMS. Each chakra sits in a specific place, has a specific color, is connected to a particular organ, and is associated with a dominant emotion. For example, the first chakra starts at the base of the body, where the legs meet the hips. This is the root chakra. Its color is red and it is based in being grounded and feeling secure in the world. These energy centers reflect and embody the wisdom of the ages which can help you find a deeper meaning in the pain or issue you are experiencing.

This chart shows each chakra and its corresponding relationship to all the principals listed above.[1]

Chakra	Location	Empowered Emotion	Color	Organ Associated
7th	Crown	Faith & Spirituality	Violet	Right Eye/ Upper Brain
6th	Third Eye	Insight, Intuition & Understanding	Indigo	Ears/ Left Eye/ Lower Brain/ Nose
5th	Throat	Communication & Speaking Your Truth	Blue	Lungs
4th	Heart	Compassion, Love & Unconditional Love	Green	Blood/ Heart
3rd	Solar Plexus	Ego, Power, Self-Esteem & Self Worth	Yellow	Gall Bladder/ Liver/ Stomach
2nd	Pelvis	Balance, Creativity & Sexuality	Orange	Reproductive System
1st	Spine (base)	Grounding The Self, Realization & Survival	Red	Kidney/ Spinal Column

1. I created this chart from many different compilations of Eastern teachings on the energy centers. Please use this chart with your own personal discretion and understand this is to help you only look in a direction and, is not to be used to give you any concrete answers.

Please refer to this chart the next time you feel any discomfort or pain in your body. This chart can give you a little guidance regarding what may be happening in your BEMS that is turning into pain. While this chart may offer guidance, it will not offer exact answers. That part is up to you, and the next step is to ask yourself questions that can give you deeper direction and insight into what your body is trying to communicate psychosomatically and then journal about what you find.

Turning Reactions into Responses

Now that we know that the difference between a reaction and response is a simple thought which is three seconds away from the stimuli, it's time to learn how to begin to choose a healthy response toward your life. It's important to recognize that feelings and emotions from the past still hurt today because of the emotional connection which is attached to the memory. To heal this, we need to deal with the past, disconnect the emotion, and then find what we want to experience **now**. This process will unlock old wounds and invite healing.

First, set some time aside and open your journal. Ask yourself the question: *"What residual pain do I feel from my past, and who hurt me?"* The goal here is to look within to find the damaging leftovers of the past, which are still hurting you today.

Next, look to see if this question triggered an image or memory, or activated any old feelings. Allow whatever comes to your mind to surface, and then write it down. Please trust whatever comes up in you, and see it as the part of your past that is now ready to heal.

Second, acknowledge which emotion this experience has unlocked. Was it abandonment? Fear? Frustration? Rejection? Focus on the actual emotion, and then begin to let go of the hurt by disconnecting that feeling from the image. So much of our suffering is held as images in our mind, but the images are painful because there is an **emotional connection** to them. Now is the time to unplug that connection from the picture in your mind.

Close your eyes, go within, and bring up that visual picture in your mind's eye. Find the cord of emotion and pull it out of the image's socket. Then, plug up that hole with some imaginary putty (so that the emotional connection can't find its way back in). Face what comes up in the process, and journal about your experience.[2]

Finally, the last step is to invite healing. After you have found your past pain and disconnected the emotional connection, it's imperative to create a new place to move into. Think of the idea of moving out of an old unpleasant house. You need to find a new house to move into, or else you would be homeless and worse off than before. You can create this new space by thinking about where you **want** to live within yourself. Just ask yourself the question, *"What do I want now?"* Journal about it, use visualization, and then create some affirmations that can help you create your new future. When you **respond** to the current circumstance, you'll continually create peace. This process will even help you rediscover your life in a positive way and, most important, do so without running to food.

As you tune in to the moment, shut off the chatter and listen when communicating with others, you'll expand your awareness and discover deeper reasons to explain why things may be happening in your life. Remember *The Rule of Three* and consciously choose to deal with your past, which will set you free in your future. Applying all these tools will continue to transform your issues with eating and help you manage your cravings. When you see pain as a messenger, life circumstances have more significance and **the continuous appetite** finally loses its power over you.

---

2. If you feel your issues run too deep and are too scary or painful to deal with alone, please seek out professional help from a Life Coach, Therapist, or Psychologist.

—Inner-Query Nine—
The Pain Journaling Questions

This exercise will help you unlock your hurt, and see how your pain might contain a deeper message to you.

A. *Get out your journal and describe what your pain feels like.*

B. *Identify WHERE the pain is in your body.*

C. *Look at the Chakra chart and find what that body part represents.*

D. *Think about how that is connected to what you may be going through.*

E. *Ask yourself the following Pain Journaling Questions:*

  1. *What information did the chart give me?*

  2. *How does the chart correlate to what's currently happening in my life?*

  3. *What is the deeper message here?*

  4. *What can I do from here on out?*

  5. *Next, go within and ask your inner self to reveal information on how you can heal your pain.*

F. *Listen for the next 24 hours for an answer.*

G. *Finally, **trust** what you find.*

If you found this exercise to be helpful,
please store it in your *Holistic Tool Box*.

114

—Chapter 10—

Unleash Your True Beauty

Acceptance and Love are the keys that unlock the
continuous appetite once and for all.

The moment you are in *right now* will have a residual effect on your future. It's important, therefore, to discuss one of the most important and powerful concepts we can embrace: **self-acceptance**.

One of the main fabrics that I have seen woven through many people's lives is the lack of self-acceptance and love, which is typically hidden under bad habits. No matter what goal you set or how much you try to accomplish, without self-acceptance, you will, unfortunately, still feel bad when you reach your destination.

I had to learn about self-acceptance the hard way. After I had lost the first sixty pounds, there would be days when I would feel like I had lost no weight at all. I'd feel physically bloated, with a sense of inner disgust toward myself, and frustrated with the small indulgent choices I'd made the night before. This would all lead me right back into the old feeling of deep self-hatred. Then I realized that, in order to truly feel good in my body, I would need to begin to practice something different: accepting it.

This concept was hard for me to understand. I'd say things like, *"I will accept myself when I arrive at my total weight loss goal, and when my body looks good."* But the mentality of thinking "when I get there" only leads you into thinking that same thing **even after you are there**. I've found that, if you truly want to be happy in your life, you need to choose to be happy **now**, regardless of your circumstance. This choice will have a residual effect when, in fact, you do actually get there.

Self-acceptance can be one of the nicest outfits you can wear. It can make you sparkle and come across to others as more genuine, and it makes them feel more comfortable as well. I've noticed that I love to be around people who are comfortable in their own skin. There is an energy about them that is so content, relaxed, and warm. It's always fulfilling to be in their presence. Do you have anyone in your life like that? I think that they are so comfortable to be with because—on a deep level—they've made the choice to accept who they are both inside and out. This ultimately creates a visible ease in the body, and other people almost always respond positively to this essence.

Are you ready to take that leap and begin practicing self-acceptance today? If so, then it's my pleasure to introduce you to one of the greatest foundations on which to live your life. This foundation is strong, it's tall, and it always supports you as it helps you hold your head up high. It gives you an inner sturdiness, exudes vitality, and speaks the wisest words. This foundation's mantra reminds you to repeat, *"I love and accept my body and myself, right **now**."* This new base is what centers you in your life and gives you the groundwork to become truly good-looking—on the inside and out. **This** is the treasure called self-acceptance, and it can do all this for **you**!

Looking Good

Being attractive, beautiful or handsome has so much more to do with what is on the inside than with what meets the eye. Think back to the time you were out and about, and noticed an attractive person. Next, recall the time when you were able to speak with that attractive person. Did this change—one way or another—your initial thoughts about their level of attraction? How was your opinion influenced by what they had to say? Did they go from a ten to a five or vice-versa?

I have had this experience go both ways. I can remember seeing an attractive man one day, then speaking with him, and being appalled by his attitude. I can also remember meeting a woman who did not strike me as beautiful but, after speaking with her, I walked away from that conversation with the warmest thoughts and feelings about her. Write down what your "surprising" experiences have been, and then reflect for a second about what changed your mind after the initial impression (because it can go from feeling someone is ugly at first to pretty). Simply said, initial attraction does **not** equal true beauty.

True beauty is so big that it fills up a room. It is bright, gentle, helpful, kind, and weightless. Beauty is acting with integrity, reliability, and respect. Beauty is a display of thoughts that empower you and, at the same time, motivate others. This type of beauty does not have a gender, but it will put a light behind your eyes and add warmth to your heart. True beauty is exuded when a spirit feels comfortable and is accepted in its own container.

This is not the type of beauty you will see on TV, or that is talked about in the tabloids. This is a deeper, longer-lasting quality that our culture could really benefit from if we could just embrace it. Do you see yourself as having America's modern-day definition of beauty or the type listed above? If you are more aligned with America's definition, the solution is simple: make a different choice!

You contain intrinsic worth, and it's time to activate this place of personal magnificence. If beauty can fill up a room, what quality is actually being exuded? It's your spirit, your own unique spiritual essence. This is who you truly are, and that "honest-self" is what people are drawn to.

To fully embrace your soul's beauty, connect to a more spiritually fulfilling outlook by linking the idea of beauty to **empowerment**, **hope**, **honor**, **insight**, **kindness**, **love**, **recognition**, **self-worth**, and **wisdom**. This will help you align your former thoughts and feelings about attractiveness to those that reflect the definition of true beauty. These are essentials that need to be on the scale whenever beauty is being weighed.

Beauty, love and acceptance can all be synonymous, and I encourage you to incorporate these concepts into your life. The Greek philosopher Plato once stated that, if you align yourself with one of the virtues, they will all line up in your life. He aligned himself with beauty and, therefore, found beauty in all things. I know you are beautiful, and the time has come for you (once and for all) to embrace your own true inner beauty.

Unconditional Love and Self-Acceptance

Unconditional love is the complete, guaranteed type of love with no limitations attached to it. This love will heal and free you from old habits and launch you into a new space of awareness where you will truly be able to identify and focus on what you want.

How do you love others? Do you love them more when they are skinnier, are wearing a nice outfit, or have accomplished something great? It's not likely, so why do we have the tendency to love ourselves with these conditions? Probably because we have this inherent counterproductive pattern of self-criticism and punishment rather than unconditional love.

If we take a look at our judicial system, one crime gets one punishment. But how many of us live in the place where one of our crimes is punished repeatedly—either in our thoughts, feelings about ourselves, or restrictions put on our lifestyle? The way to end this negative cycle is to begin to notice all the things we punish ourselves for and then create a little wiggle room so we can practice unconditional love.

The summary I use to describe **unconditional love** is: *acceptance without boundaries, kindness without a goal, and patience without expectations.* Let's break this down:

Acceptance without Boundaries

Acceptance is an attitude that sounds like, *"Everything is okay right now!"* This place of "being okay" is receiving the moment for all it is, being present, and then making the choice to allow it to flow in or out of you, without judgment.

Kindness without a Goal

Kindness is a thoughtful generosity that comes from the purest intentions and starts deep within the heart. When kindness flows without a goal, the outcome creates a compassionate environment.

Patience without Expectations

Patience is an inner endurance to gracefully wait for something's arrival. This serenity comes from a place of love and a dwelling from within.

Unconditional love already exists within all of us but, as the storms of life rain upon us, the heart can become callused. Does your heart feel hardened? If so, are you ready to let that tough shell melt away? Begin by answering what your specific thoughts and feelings are toward love:

- *When you hear the word love, what image comes to mind?*
- *When you feel loved, what memories are triggered?*
- *If love provokes any negative feelings, are you ready to heal those parts of you?*
- *How can you begin—today—to give yourself more unconditional love?*

Remember, you have to get rid of the old in order to make room for the new and these questions will help you unlock your old patterns to create a new inner space. As you become more aware and conscious of how you haven't loved or accepted yourself, you can clear out the old and begin to refill that space with what feels good.

The Language of Acceptance

How we speak and what we say is a reflection of what we think. Paying attention to our language is the next step toward unleashing true beauty, which is acceptance and unconditional love. The words we currently use show us what we think about. And what we think about is usually created through our beliefs, which lie deeper within us and create our perspective on life. Becoming mentally aware of our language will help us begin to embrace our true inner beauty. Please listen for these specific phrases in your language, eliminate them, and then practice inserting the new suggestion.

Should

Whenever you use the word **should** you are unconsciously putting yourself in a powerless position which requires defense. Instead, try substituting the word **could**. This will give you your power back and show you all the possibility and action you can take in your life. For example if you say to yourself, *"I should have gone to the grocery store,"* how does this sentence make you feel? Does it make you feel bad, disempowered, like a failure, or like a loser? If you change it to **could** it would sound like this, *"I could have gone to the grocery store... but I didn't because I was too tired."* How does this make you feel? Maybe that there was a good reason that you made that choice? **Should** implies regret; while **could** implies choice. Begin to eliminate the word **should** from your language, and instead begin to replace it with **could**.

I Don't Want...

When I ask my clients what it is that they want, eight out of ten people first respond with something like, *"Well, I don't want to be stressed, in debt or have conflict."* But I didn't ask them what they DON'T want; I asked them what they DO want. It's important to become aware of all your thoughts about what you don't want, because this can then show you that you need to look in a different direction.

When you notice that all you're thinking about is what you DON'T want, start to ask yourself what the opposite is, and what it is that you DO want. Notice how much you talk about what you DON'T want and then change the sentence to reflect what you DO want.

It's Too Difficult / It's a Problem

These phrases are from the perspective of defeat. Exit the defeat mentality and enter the growth mentality. Anytime you see something as a "problem" or "too difficult", try replacing it with **growth opportunity,** or **being brave,** or **a developmental chance**. This puts you in a power position to become ready to grow in the situation and to become a better you. For example if you say, *"I lost my job and it's too difficult to find another one,"* the other side of this perspective could be, *"I have this developmental chance to figure out what I really want to do, act brave, and accept this growth opportunity to become all I need to be to land my dream job."*

View the words that come from your mouth as the crumbs that are falling from your mind. By paying attention to your expressions, language, and vocabulary, you'll be waking up your mind, expanding your mental awareness, and sharpening your intellect. As you replace these old habits, your brain will begin to see the direction you are now trying to grow in.

As you begin to accept yourself, love yourself unconditionally, and change your communication skills, you'll have the result of diffusing **the continuous appetite** once and for all.

—Inner-Query Ten—

The Love List

"20 Things You LOVE About Yourself"

The point of this exercise is to help you acknowledge all that you currently have that is beautiful and loveable, as well as to help your conscious mind begin to embrace these things within.

A. *Get out your journal or blank sheet of paper.*

B. *Write down 20 things that you LOVE about yourself.*

C. *Read it daily.*

D. *Continue to add ten things to this list every week.*

E. *Keep this on-going list in your journal.*

If you found this exercise to be helpful,
please store it in your *Holistic Tool Box.*

—Chapter 11—
Events, Holidays
& Vacations

Knowing how to sample food and not let continuous eating override
the system is a priceless life skill that will continually reward you.

I once had a client say to me, "Eating season begins on Halloween with a huge bowl of candy in my lap and goes through New Year's Eve where I finally make my resolution to—once again—lose weight." Does this sound familiar? If so, you no longer need to follow this faulty pattern. Events, holidays, and vacations are the times when we are supposed to enjoy food and indulge ourselves a little more. When we live in a tumultuous relationship with food, however, it can make these celebratory times seem like a drag.

Birthdays, events, holidays, and vacations are the times when you are supposed to treat yourself and enjoy the yummy—albeit not so healthy—foods. The smart way to embrace this concept is to have a daily, balanced eating regimen so that when these occasions do pop up, you can **calmly plan ahead and then enjoy them**.

I'm guessing that, by now, you have an eating plan that you follow which works for you. In Chapter 6, you were given a couple of eating tips to apply to your daily eating regimen and, then asked to incorporate the ones you had synergy with into your life. Hopefully, you've been following an approach that is working for you. The next step is to learn how to be at an event, enjoy the holidays, or even go on a vacation and still have balance when it comes to what you eat.

The 80/20 Rule

The **80/20 Rule** is the idea that, eighty percent of the time, eating is for fuel and, twenty percent of the time, eating is slightly more indulgent. Before you attend an event, find yourself in the middle of the holiday season, or go on a vacation, it's imperative to understand this 80/20 Rule because it can shed insight into what overeating actually does to your body.

When these percentages are broken down over a week, the ratio would reflect 5.6 days of eating that would be for fuel and 1.4 days that could be more indulgent. In real time, this means Sunday through Friday afternoon would be devoted to eating healthy and whole foods in order to fuel your body's needs, while Friday night and Saturday could be more indulgent.

This 80/20 Rule illustrates just why gaining weight from the holiday season or from being on vacation is so prevalent. Those times are when eating has more of a 50/50 ratio (fuel/pleasure) or—even worse—a 20/80 ratio. Either way, it's imperative to know how to handle yourself with the 80/20 Rule **before** you are at an event or embark upon a vacation where you're surrounded by tempting, indulgent foods.

Of course, the balance you'll need for a weekend wedding celebration is going to be very different from the ratio you would need for a ten-day cruise.

Finding Your Ratio

The first step is to look back at your eating habits during a normal day to see what your current percentages are with fuel versus fun food. Get out a piece of paper and draw two columns, one for Fuel and one for Pleasure. Then write down all the foods you eat during the week in the appropriate column. After doing the simple math, there would ideally be 80 items in the fuel column and 20 items in the pleasure column. This "accounting" will help you become aware of what your fuel to pleasure ratio is.

Creating Your Plan

The next step is to create a reasonable eating *plan* for the event, holiday, or vacation that is somewhat close to your current ratio. This might mean that, if your current numbers are 65/35 (on a daily basis), then set the goal to eat 50/50 at the occasion. In reality, this would then represent that, for every treat you enjoyed, you would have a whole food like a green vegetable before or afterward. Once you have created a plan, the final step is to just follow the path you've laid out for yourself while you are at the event, enjoying the holiday season, or on vacation.

Events

We all have busy lives that require us to attend many functions that pop up throughout the year. An event would be considered an occasion that happens during a 24-hour period, and then it's over. These would be considered in-town affairs that don't require travel, such as: anniversaries, birthdays, celebrating a friend's promotion, charity functions, happy hours, house parties, social engagements, in-town weddings, etc. The length of these events is important, because it can help guide the way you plan your eating strategy for the subsequent and prior weeks.

Obviously, the best way to have success with anything is to a) first prepare a plan, and then b) execute with action. Begin by looking at the year in advance, and note all the planned occurrences like anniversaries, birthdays, and the set occasions you have already committed to within the next twelve months. As you take an authentic look at all the events scheduled in your life (most of which are probably focused around food), it's easier to see some of the potential road blocks **before** they derail you onto an overeating detour. This approach alone will help you see what is on your social horizon so that you prepare a plan in advance. That way, when the event comes around, you'll be prepared to take action and execute your plan while attending the event.

Before I followed this approach to the events in my life, I'd often feel as if, right when I (finally) got my eating back on track, another event would throw me for a loop. I would then go to the event, totally blow my diet, leave the event feeling bad about myself, and repeat the same sentence each time: *"I will start my diet on Monday."* If this scenario seems familiar to you, you can change it by simply looking ahead and creating a workable plan.

When it comes to events, the 80/20 Rule in its simplest form is: **eat healthy all week and then enjoy yourself at the event.** The indulgent experience at the event can easily account for that twenty percent and, because you have planned for it, you can avoid feeling guilty. Events are the appropriate venue to savor food and, in order to truly enjoy, you need to have a balanced diet throughout the week. Once the event is over, the very next morning is the time to return to your healthy eating track.

It can be so simple. First, find an eating plan that works for you, understand the 80/20 ratio of fuel to pleasure, (eat healthy eighty percent of the time), look at what you have going on in your social life, make an eating plan before each event and, while at the event, execute the plan so that you can enjoy every moment.

Holidays

In American culture, there is a holiday to celebrate within every month, starting with New Years Day and continuing through Valentine's Day, St. Patrick's Day, Easter, Mother's Day, Memorial Day, Father's Day, Fourth of July, Labor Day, Halloween, Thanksgiving, and Christmas. This is not including all the other holidays from different religions and cultures that are sprinkled into the mix! Additionally, there are friends' birthdays and family gatherings that are celebrated throughout the year.

Typically in our culture we celebrate through eating and drinking and if we tally all these holidays together over a year, the total is slightly more than one holiday per month! This means that, if you have one event per month and one holiday per month, half of your weekends will be spent in overindulgence. This is fine if that is how you choose to use the 80/20 Rule, but the problem is that most people let the holiday mentality bleed into the week, which results in more of a 40/60 ratio and translates into weight gain.

It doesn't, however, have to be this way. Overindulgent holidays can be counterbalanced by having a daily intention to be healthier both before and after the holiday, and then by following these tips on the day of the holiday:

- Look at the holidays as a one-day event.
- Commit to following the 80/20 Rule from October through January.

- On a holiday:
  - Wake up and move your body for 30 minutes.
  - Plan what you will eat throughout the day and then follow that plan.
  - Eat normal meals throughout the day.
  - Eating on the holiday:
  - Choose to eat the foods you LOVE (if you put something into your mouth and don't love it, don't eat the rest).
  - Chew every bite, at least, twenty times.
  - Pick one appetizer, have one serving, put it on a plate and sit down to enjoy it.
  - Decide to have only one type of meat, with the serving no larger than the palm of your hand.
  - Say "NO" to seconds!
  - Have a 2-3 alcoholic drink maximum.
  - Select one dessert to eat, sit down to eat it, and enjoy every bite!

Holidays are a time of celebration, and it's okay to taste and enjoy, but try not to overindulge. After the day is over, return to your normal eating regimen. Remember, if you know how to enjoy the flavor of food, you won't need to keep placing more into your mouth because more never tastes better. It is just more.

Vacations

A vacation is a period of time devoted to recreation, rest, or travel. For the sake of this chapter, a vacation would be defined as time away from your normal life that exceeds three days. The average American vacation is about one or two weeks per year and, typically, vacationers come home more exhausted than when they left. The overindulgent, overdoing mentality tends to rear its ugly head during vacations because so many of us simply don't know how to stop and relax. Look at the numbers. We only take a few days each year to figure out how to pause our busy lives, so we are not well-versed in stopping. This limitation then keeps us on overdrive and, if our past habit is to overdo it with food, then we'll find ourselves once again overeating while on vacation.

The purpose of going on a vacation is to take a break, enjoy a retreat, relax, and forget about that never-ending to-do list. We need, therefore, to be conscious of not overdoing it in the food department because this will immediately take us out of a restful state and into a stressful state, which is definitely not the point of being on vacation. The 80/20 Rule is not a "law" on vacation, but rather a "helpful reminder" to support you to not overindulge. Remember that, when you overeat, you don't feel good and if you're on vacation, I'll bet you probably want to feel really **great**.

When you're eating on vacation, keep this question in mind: *"If I eat this food, will I feel good?"* Allow the truthful answer to surface, and then make your choice. If the answer is "no" and you still want the food, have it, but train yourself to take only three bites and then leave the rest. (The trained act of taking three bites will expand in you as you practice dealing with the issues underneath your cravings by asking *The Four Questions*). This act of control over food will then leave you feeling good in your body, your mouth, and your self-esteem.

I have noticed that, when people make the shift into choosing to feel good in their body over immediate gratification in their mouth, **the final result is always weight loss.** Keep in mind that it is okay to gain a couple of pounds on vacation, but try to never gain more than three pounds total. If you want to stay even more disciplined while on vacation, get a scale that can travel with you and step on it each morning to keep yourself accountable. Here are a few more tips to help you stay balanced while on vacation:

- If you overeat one day, simply admit it to yourself, exercise a little longer the following day, and order fruit and vegetables with all your meals.
- Drink plenty of water.
- Take naps.
- If you overeat, brush your teeth. This will psychologically help you not want to put anything else in your mouth.
- Weigh yourself before you leave as well as on the morning after you return.
- Don't be upset with a little weight gain; just use that number as valuable information to show you *the result of your food choices*, and then clean up your eating habits ASAP!

Be honest with yourself and know that a small weight gain on vacation is normal. It is, however, essential for you to make the commitment to return to your healthy eating regimen the morning after you get back home. The most important thing you can do after a vacation is be straightforward with yourself, get back on track, and support yourself during the process of regaining control.

All Inclusive Cruises

Have you ever been on an all-inclusive cruise? This is where any and all food—in any amount—is available twenty-four hours a day. This "inclusive" fact will encourage **the continuous appetite** to come out and play. Over-indulgence, however, will **never** make you feel good and, if you don't want to spend your time on (or after) a cruise feeling bad, learn to be moderate with the buffet.

The goal is to enjoy the food—without overdoing it—by sticking to three meals a day that are the size of your two palms put together. Think about what is on your plate and then imagine pouring all the food from your plate into your hands. Could they hold it all? This is a good image to keep you more balanced when it comes to the endless temptations that an all-inclusive cruise offers.

Next, we have to go over this mentality: *"It's free and available, so I must eat it."* The first thing to recognize here is that, when you are on an all-inclusive cruise, it doesn't mean that you have to eat the ship. It means that the food is a *piece* of what you are paying for; only a **piece**. Your money is paying for the overall experience of the voyage, the electricity, the staff, the gas, your rooms, the ship's décor, and all that it costs to get you to and from your destinations. The food costs are just a small portion of this.

Usually, these "all-inclusive" deals don't even include alcohol. Why is that? Because the cost margin for alcohol is higher than food and the ship's owners know they can make more money on alcohol than they ever could on food, so they charge for drinks. I encourage you to remember that, anytime you catch yourself reasoning, *"It's free and available, so I must eat it"*, this is a misleading thought. Think about the other things that your money is paying for, step away from the buffet table, and learn to enjoy the moment.

Buffets

Think of a buffet filled with various amounts of foods set out for you to take (serve yourself at any time and quantity). Many people struggle with buffets because they are able to have whatever they feel like (in heaping amounts, whenever they want), for the entirety of the trip. This can cause people to go into a continuous eating zone that makes it hard to find the "off" mechanism. For most people, this can be dangerous, so here are a couple of tips to remember when approaching a buffet:

- Visually scan the buffet **before** you grab a plate.
- Make the commitment to go to the buffet only once.
- Grab one plate and mentally think of separating it into three sections: a green vegetable, protein, and carbohydrate.
- Start with the green vegetable first, then pick a veggie dish or salad and fill one third of your plate with that choice.
- Next, choose the type of protein (meat, eggs, etc.) you'd like that is no larger than your hand, and fill the next third of your plate with your selection.
- Finally, choose your carbohydrate, and place it on the last third of your plate.
- Then go to your table, sit down, exhale deeply, and order a seltzer water.
- Finally, if you like dessert, choose one, sit down and enjoy every bite you take.
- Remember: Do not eat what you don't like; just push it to the side of your plate.

Feeling good on a vacation is priceless, and overeating can be a costly mistake. Gaining a few pounds during an event, the holidays, or on a vacation is normal but, to truly feel great while away, have a plan beforehand, follow the path you've laid out for yourself, and then do your personal best.

The 24-Hour Rule

After an event or holiday, it can be hard to switch off the indulgent mechanism because the body had been overloaded with fat, salt, and sugar—which, unfortunately, makes you feel like you want more of the same. If you have gained weight during one of these occasions, it's what I like to call *easy fat* or *soft fat* because it has not yet turned into hard fat. The timing here is crucial because, in my experience, easy fat turns into hard fat in about seven days. Therefore, it's fundamental to get right back into your healthy eating regimen within twenty-four hours after your festive event, holiday, or vacation.

These twenty-four hours are about making the transition from indulgent to clean eating, simply by being intentional. Here are a couple of tips to help you achieve this:

- Plan out your meals for the week ahead of time: breakfast, lunch, dinner, and two snacks for each day.
- EX: For breakfast: egg whites and toast. Three hours later: a banana. For Lunch: an open-face turkey sandwich. Three hours later: an apple. For dinner: a chicken breast, half a cup of black beans, and spinach.
- Go to the store and only buy what is on the list (even if there are great sales on other items).
- If you feel the need to eat outside of meal time, drink seltzer water.
- Prepare your dinners for one week, in one setting. Refrain from munching while cooking.
- Once the meals are ready, measure out appropriate portions and place into separate Tupperware containers. Then label them: Monday, Tuesday, etc.
- When eating throughout the week, place your food on a small salad plate, heat up your meal, and then sit down to eat.
- Eat in a calm space and consciously breathe between bites.
- When cleaning up, chew gum.

- If you need a sweet fix; eat one serving of dark chocolate chips.
- If you feel hungry after eating, drink seltzer water and go for a 10-20 minute walk to help your body move and to process the food.
- Hungry before bed? Just go to sleep, grab a book and begin to shut down your engine. It's better for the body to not process food when sleeping.

Remember, you are steering your appetite away from overindulgence and into health, and this may cause you to temporarily feel a little hungry. But that's okay. The simple act of being intentional is the difference between once being controlled by the continuous appetite and now being in control of your appetite. As you transition from processing fatty and salty treats to processing clean foods instead, there will be a physiological shift from feeling bad to feeling good.

Food is for fuel but God also gave us taste buds and when we mindfully enjoy an event, holiday, or vacation, we are balancing food's purpose of fuel and pleasure. Knowing how to sample food and not let continuous eating override the system is a priceless life skill which will continually reward you.

—Inner-Query Eleven—

The Feel Good Collage

The idea behind this exercise is to put positive energy into creating what you want and to get in touch with experiencing how that feels. This is great to do on a vacation because you can begin to look through magazines and collect images that make you feel good. The result of all these images can be called your vision board, manifestation book, dream collection, etc.

A. *Cut out, clip and save pictures, words, articles of or about things that make you feel good.*

B. *Place all these items in one space and, when you have about 20 items total, begin to build your collage and, then paste it to a poster board.*

C. *Hang this collage where you can see it and look at it on a daily basis.*

D. *Next, as you go through your day, look for things that inspire a positive response in you and feel it fully!*

If you found this exercise to be helpful,
please store it in your *Holistic Tool Box*.

—Chapter 12—
Discover Your Best Self

*Through the transformation of your Body, Emotions, Mind,
and Spirit, the continuous appetite has finally vanished.*

All the work you have done up to this point is why your continuous appetite is vanishing. The effort you've put into practicing the plethora of exercises outlined so far has now made you aware of the three different categories that food falls into: cravings, favorite foods, and hunger. After your familiarity continues to expand, you'll easily be able to decipher which category you are dealing with, and this will lead you to the final step of overcoming **the continuous appetite**.

Cravings

When you're having a craving, it's important to remember to do the inner work. Cravings typically mean that something is out of balance within and it's trying to get your attention. This means that you now have the opportunity to take five minutes to look at yourself—instead of running to food—and ask *The Four Questions*. This effort will help you see what is happening beneath the surface so that you can address and then transform the real issue. Just remember: to find the answer, you first have to ask the question!

Favorite Foods

When you want your favorite food, first ask yourself what you think this food is going to do for you. If you get an answer that states, *"I want to enjoy the taste in my mouth"* or *"I can be satisfied within the first three bites,"* then have an appropriate amount of the food. On the other hand, if you get the indication that you just want to temporarily feel better, then it's time to look within and find out what is off balance. After you check in and go through this process, you can then ask yourself if you still want to eat your favorite food and, if the answer is *"yes"*, go for it.

Hunger

When you are hungry, it's key to fuel the body with whole and healthy foods, plain and simple. This is the easiest part, because all you have to do at this point is follow the eating plan you have synergy with and enjoy the gentle outcome of feeling healthy.

The Four Steps to Getting What You Want

I want to make sure that you understand that you **can have** whatever you want in this lifetime. You no longer need to be controlled by feeling bad in your BEMS, which may have felt like unhealthiness in your body, instability in your emotions, defeating negative thoughts, or a disconnection from your truest spiritual source. Now is the time to pave your future and bring yourself what you DO WANT.

The way to receiving your desires is to first **discover** what they are. Next, you must believe that these desires are whispers from your heart to your head, which eventually help you live and fulfill your life's purpose. Once you're aware of your inner desire, you can then move to the other stages of manifestation. This process will help you become clear with what is going on inside of you and what you need to do to turn your desires into reality. The four components to create what you DO want in your life are **desire**, **deserve**, **ask**, and **know**.

Desire

This is the way that things show up to us, and it's the first part of creation. The internal dialogue might sound like this: *"I wish I could lose weight, be skinnier, or more muscular."* We have to be in touch with what we want, in order to be able to notice it once it shows up. The *desire* stage is vital to bringing anything you want into your life. So what do you truly desire?

Deserve

Do you believe, deep down in your heart of hearts, that you *deserve* to have the thing you desire? The second step is checking in with your inner life and asking if you believe that you *deserve* it. This stage is crucial because, if you don't feel you **deserve** it, you will just stay in the wishing stage. If your answer is, *"Yes, I do deserve it,"* then you can move along to the next stage. If, however, the answer is *"no"*, you must do some inner work to uncover the emotions and thoughts that are making you feel that you **don't** deserve this thing. In order to move forward, it's imperative to unblock yourself from undeserving beliefs. Do you believe that you deserve to have what you desire?

Ask

Asking is the enthusiastic planning stage where you *request* the thing you desire and deserve. The *"ask"* is done with intention, willingness and determination from a deep place within. Jesus said, "Ask and you shall receive." There is a lot of power in these five words strung together. There is magnificent support that happens once we really put our intention out there. Your desire might sound like: *"I really want to lose weight and am ready to begin a new eating plan."* The **ask** portion of this **desire** then might sound like: *"God, please guide me to the perfect weight loss plan, help me truly heal the issues that put this weight on, and gracefully support me as it melts away."* How can **you** open up and ask the universe for what you want?

Know

Once you *know* it, it will manifest. The final step to getting what you want is by putting emotional passion into it by knowing and believing that you can have anything you desire. By going into an inner space and feeling, thinking, and acting as if it's already here, you begin to draw this desire toward you. When you *know* something, it comes from a place of profound inner awareness. *Knowing* is the stage which requires faith and patience, and it happens right before things manifest. Practice these four steps to bring your inner desires into reality.

<u>Discover Your Best Self</u>

Life is a continuous class and, if we don't ask the questions, we will never find the answers. When we don't have the answers, we end up living out our lives by walking in circles and repeating the same class. To prevent a circular existence, it is essential to know that you have the power—already within you—to create a life that you would love to live.

Take this day and think in terms of how you would like it to go. What would you like to happen, feel, or experience? Open your journal and write it out. Then turn all your negative chatter, tasks, or worries into an opportunity and look at them as if there is a message lying underneath, trying to lead you to a greater place.

Learning to uncover "your best" on a daily basis is a practice, and sometimes all it takes is the awareness of what your best is—right here, right now—in this very moment. Once you find your best, you can give it back to the world, and that is a great feeling. The following questions will help you develop and stay on track to living your best life and will enhance your life journey. Ask yourself these six questions today, and then revisit them in a year:

1. *Who am I?*
2. *What does integrity mean to me and how can I practice that?*
3. *What have I been through that has taught me great lessons?*
4. *What do I want to do with my life?*
5. *Where do I see myself a year from today?*
6. *How can I get there?*

I encourage you to face the challenges that life offers you and to see them as an opportunity to grow into your best self. When a growth opportunity comes your way, use the tools you've learned in this book, practice looking within to locate your suffering, and then choose to turn that pain into inner awareness.

The Process Simplified

Life will always present us with storms. In the past, these storms may have caused overeating but, now, you have an umbrella of exercises and techniques to keep you dry. You have the power to live the life you want rather than be controlled by **the continuous appetite**. Whenever you feel a little out of balance, just remember the key points:

❖ Food is not the problem.

❖ Whenever you are tempted to overeat ask and answer *The Four Questions*:

1. *What happened today?*
2. *What emotion was I feeling?*
3. *What does this feel like within?*
4. *What do I want to feel?*

❖ Write in your journal, and figure out what you DO WANT in your life.

❖ Face yourself and answer the five *Escape Pattern Questions:*

1. *What was happening when I chose to overeat?*
2. *What did I do to handle the situation?*
3. *What emotion did the circumstances make me feel?*
4. *What other things can I do when I feel that same emotion?*
5. *When I find myself in this situation again, what can my future-self do instead of eat?*

❖ Eat every three hours and, if eating out, **Eat Half, Leave Half!**

❖ Truly taste the first three bites.

❖ Know that YOU are the only true **power** in your world.

❖ Recognize the three levels of the mind and silence the **Chatter**, find solutions through clear **Cognition**, and choose to live in **The Now**.

❖ Remember *The Rule of Three* and why things happen in life:

1. *It is an answered prayer in disguise*
2. *It is The Law of Attraction manifesting*
3. *It is a life lesson*

❖ Practice self-acceptance and love, as these are the keys to a happy life.

❖ Plan ahead before you go to an event, have a holiday or go on vacation.

These are the tools I keep in my *Holistic Tool Box*; and they have changed my relationship with food and my transformed my life. My hope is that you have begun to see that you, too, can live the life you want.

One last step along this path is remembering to be grateful for your body. Your body is an amazing machine that continues to provide millions of miracles—day in and day out—without a single conscious thought. Now is the time to recognize your miraculous body and say, "Thank you!" Begin to look at your astounding body in a way where you see your blemishes as your body's intuitive equilibrium trying to find balance, your cellulite as your intricate animal pattern that only you have, your scars as reminders of how you've gained wisdom, and your so-called imperfections as unique distinctions that make you—YOU. Please begin to use your thoughts to give your body conscious appreciation. This practice will lead you to true well-being, which is always available to us through awareness. After you are grateful for your body, you can then practice being **grateful** for who you are.

As you say goodbye to continuous eating, make the conscious effort to say hello to your best self. **Acceptance**, **freedom**, and **harmony** can now be the strings on your guitar but the journey does not end here, as this is only a lyric in your life song. The next time you have a craving, a bad thought, or an unconformable condition, remember that you have the knowledge to know how to handle this. Please choose to love your body, acknowledge your emotions, transform your thoughts, and listen to your spirit. If you can do this, your holistic makeover will be complete. Through the transformation of your Body, Emotions, Mind, and Spirit, **the continuous appetite** has finally vanished! Congratulations—you have found your inner freedom!

—Inner-Query Twelve—
The Complete Holistic Tool Box

You did it! You walked down a courageous path that has hopefully brought you great insight.

    A. *Take all the exercises you have practiced that were effective and arrange them in your toolbox so that they can be helpful in your future.*

    B. *Keep your toolbox in a place that is safe but convenient for future life storms.*

    C. *Feel the completion of this journey.*

    D. *Breathe in completion and exhale your success!*

Please enjoy your *Holistic Tool Box* and use it whenever you find yourself in a challenging life situation.

Remember:

"Life is like the ocean, you can't stop the waves, but you can learn to surf."
-Jon Kabat Zin

"You don't have to see the whole staircase...

...just take the first step."

-Martin Luther King Jr.

About the Author

Sophie Skover is an author, holistic life coach, inspirational speaker and intuitive teacher, who works to help others experience harmony in their lives. She became passionate about this "life changing" path after she healed from bulimia and lost seventy-five pounds through the process.

Sophie believes, and has seen through her own experience, that you can heal from anything that comes your way. As she healed her own inner issues, one craving at a time, she developed a program to heal what she calls The Continuous Appetite™. This helps people who emotionally overeat to transform the body, emotions, mind, and spirit by gently pulling back the layers of dysfunction when a craving surfaces.

In 2006, Sophie started her own company, LSS Harmony Life Coaching, to help people who are struggling with life to find freedom. She works with clients, conducts workshops, practices yoga, and runs every morning with her dog Jack. She currently lives in West Palm Beach, Florida and encourages us to face our inner life and grow into the most impressive version of ourselves.

For more information, please visit

www.LSSHarmony.com

If this book had any transformational impact on your life,
we would love to hear from you. Please send us your story:
info@LSSHarmony.com

Printed in the United States
By Bookmasters